I0800939

CLASSICAL COMICS

TEACHING RESOURCE PACK

Making the classics accessible
for teachers and students

Suitable for teaching ages 10-17

Written by: Gareth Calway
US Adaptation: Joe Sutliff Sanders

Jane Eyre

THE GRAPHIC NOVEL

Charlotte Brontë

CLASSICAL COMICS TEACHING RESOURCE PACK

Jane Eyre: The Graphic Novel

First US Edition
Published by: Classical Comics Ltd

Written by: Gareth Calway
US Adaptation: Joe Sutliff Sanders
Artwork: John M. Burns
Design & Layout: Jo Wheeler & Carl Andrews
Editor in Chief: Clive Bryant

Acknowledgments: Every effort has been made to trace copyright holders of material reproduced in this book. Any rights not acknowledged here will be acknowledged in subsequent editions if notice is given to Classical Comics Ltd.

All enquiries should be addressed to:
Classical Comics Ltd.
PO Box 7280
Litchborough
Towcester
NN12 9AR
United Kingdom
Tel: +44 (0)845 812 3000

education@classicalcomics.com
www.classicalcomics.com

ISBN: 978-1-906332-55-6

Printed in the UK

CONTENTS

INTRODUCTION

WELCOME TO THE *JANE EYRE* TEACHING RESOURCE FROM CLASSICAL COMICS.

As always with our teaching resources we aim to provide enough information to satisfy teachers and students alike, in the form of enjoyable activities that children will engage with. The exercises are designed to be used to teach students between 10 and 17 years old. They can be adapted to suit the needs of your classroom and customized to meet most skill levels. Our focus is, as always, on fun as well as learning.

This resource can be used alongside the Classical Comics adaptation of *Jane Eyre* as well as a traditional text, although that definitely isn't a requirement. In fact, many of the activities can stand on their own as introductions to the world of the Brontës.

You will see opportunities for cross-curricular study including history, drama and art.

A varied selection of activities will ensure that many aspects of speaking and listening, reading and writing are covered – whatever age group you are teaching.

This photocopiable resource is designed with ease of use in mind. If you would like to send feedback to improve this book, please email info@classicalcomics.com.

Your thoughts and input are always appreciated.

Classical Comics Ltd

Gareth Calway taught in secondary schools (the name given to High Schools in the UK) for 27 years, leading departments for twelve of them. He is now a NATE (the National Association for the Teaching of English) consultant who regularly runs workshops and seminars at NATE conferences, as well as touring workshops to schools at all stages. He has written and published resources for English (and media) since *Creative Language* in the late 80s, often specializing in poetry and the Victorian novel. He is a regular resource writer for Oxford University Press's *Rollercoaster* Series, producing detailed schemes of work for popular novels. He is a series writer and editor for Harper Collins resources and contributed to Hodder's *Living Literature and Language* series. He is an examiner for exam boards in England and Wales. Apart from English, he has led drama and expressive arts departments, founded and led a media studies department and taught lots of history. Since "retiring" he has published a comic novel about schooldays called *River Deep Mountain High*. His one-man show *Tales Out Of School* played at the 2007 Edinburgh Fringe Festival, and he continues to tour shows as well as offer workshops to schools.

CHARLOTTE BRONTË 1816 – 1855

"Literature cannot be the business of a woman's life..."
Poet Laureate Robert Southey's letter to Charlotte Brontë in 1837

George Richmond, chalk, 1850 National Portrait Gallery, London

Charlotte Brontë was born on April 21, 1816, at 74 Market Street in the village of Thornton near Bradford, Yorkshire. She was one of six children born to Maria Branwell and Patrick Brontë: Maria (1814), Elizabeth (1815), Charlotte (1816), Patrick Branwell (who was known as Branwell, 1817), Emily (1818) and Anne (1820).

Her father, Patrick, was an Irish Anglican clergyman and writer born in County Down, Ireland, in 1777. His surname was originally Brunty, but he decided to change his name, probably to give the impression of a more well-to-do background, giving the world the now familiar "Brontë." Charlotte's mother, Maria, was born in 1785, to a prosperous merchant family in Cornwall. Patrick and Maria met in Hartshead, Yorkshire, while she was helping her aunt with the domestic side of running a school.

In April 1820, when Charlotte was four years old, the family moved a short distance from Thornton to Haworth, where Patrick had been appointed perpetual curate of the church. Maria's sister Elizabeth joined them a year later to help look after the children and to care for her sister, who was suffering from the final stages of cancer. Maria died in September 1821 – Charlotte was still only five years old.

The Parsonage at Haworth was a literary household. From early childhood, the Brontë children had written about the lives, wars and sufferings of people who lived in their own imaginary kingdoms. The story goes that Branwell had been given a set of toy soldiers in June 1826, and from these the children developed imaginary worlds of their own. Charlotte and Branwell wrote stories about their country — "Angria" — and Emily and Anne wrote articles and poems about theirs — "Gondal". These sagas, plays, poems and stories were written down in handmade "little books" — books that they made from paper sheets stitched together. In a letter to author and biographer Elizabeth Gaskell, Patrick Brontë wrote:

> "When mere children, as soon as they could read and write, Charlotte and her brother and sisters used to invent and act little plays of their own."

In July 1824 Maria (ten) and Elizabeth (nine) were sent to the Clergy Daughter's School at Cowan Bridge, near Kirkby Lonsdale in Lancashire. Charlotte (eight) and Emily (six) joined them there in August. Life at boarding school must have been grim. Maria became ill and was sent home in February 1825; she died at Haworth in May. Elizabeth fell ill that same month and, like her sister, was sent home; she died just a few months later. Both sisters died of tuberculosis (also known as "consumption"), and as a result of their deaths, Emily and Charlotte were withdrawn from the school. These events obviously had a great impact on Charlotte, who drew on the experience for *Jane Eyre* when she described Lowood School and the death of Helen Burns.

In fact much of the novel mirrors Charlotte's own life. Charlotte, like Jane, spent many years as a governess for a number of families – a career which she viewed with some distaste. Having no personal fortune and few respectable ways of earning a living, this was the only socially acceptable option for many genteel young ladies. Emily and Anne also became governesses, although Emily's career as a

CHARLOTTE BRONTË

teacher was short-lived; it is reported that she told her pupils at Miss Patchett's School in Halifax that she much preferred the school dog to any of them! In 1842, Charlotte and Emily travelled to Brussels to study at the Pensionnat Heger – a boarding school run by Constantin Heger and his wife. Their aunt Elizabeth Branwell paid for this trip, with the plan that they would set up their own school at the Parsonage when they returned. However, the girls were forced to return to England later that year

when Aunt Elizabeth died – just as in this book when Jane Eyre returns to Gateshead Hall when her Aunt Reed is on her death-bed. Charlotte traveled alone to Brussels in January 1843 to take up a teaching post at Pensionnat Heger. This second stay was not a happy one: she was lonely without her sister, homesick, and increasingly attached to Constantin Heger. She returned to Haworth a year later in January 1844. Her time at Pensionnat Heger became the inspiration for parts of two other books: *The Professor* and *Villette*. Her attraction to the married Constantin would seem to reflect Jane Eyre's love for Mr. Rochester.

Of the three sisters, Anne was the most successful teacher; but by 1845 the entire family, including Branwell, were all back at The Parsonage. Branwell returned home somewhat in disgrace for "proceedings bad beyond expression" – most likely a love affair with his employer's wife.

After Charlotte's return home, the sisters finally started on their project to start a school of their own. This turned out to be a total failure – they didn't manage to attract a single student! However, that was probably to the world's advantage. Over the years, the sisters had continued their writing, and in 1846 – having abandoned the idea of starting a school – they decided to publish a selection of their poems. The title was simply *Poems,* and it was published under different author names: Currer (Charlotte), Ellis (Emily) and Acton (Anne) Bell. One thousand copies of the book were printed, at a cost of around £50, which they funded themselves. The book received some favorable reviews, but it sold only two copies in the first year.

Charlotte gave an explanation for these pseudonyms:

> "Averse to personal publicity, we veiled our own names under those of Currer, Ellis and Acton Bell; the ambiguous choice being dictated by a sort of conscientious scruple at assuming Christian names positively masculine, while we did not like to declare ourselves women, because – without at that time suspecting that our mode of writing and thinking was not what is called "feminine" – we had a vague impression that authoresses are liable to be looked on with prejudice; we had noticed how critics sometimes use for their chastisement the weapon of personality, and for their reward, a flattery, which is not true praise."

In the same year that *Poems* was published, Charlotte also completed her first novel, *The Professor*. It was rejected by a number of publishers, but despite that, Charlotte remained undeterred. The following year saw the publication of Charlotte's *Jane Eyre*, Emily's *Wuthering Heights*, and Anne's *Agnes Grey*; all published under their assumed "Bell" names. The sisters hid behind their assumed names until 1848, when Anne's second novel, *The Tenant of Wildfell Hall* was published, and the sisters were forced to reveal their true identities.

These first successes for the sisters were overshadowed by sadness. Their brother, Branwell, had been subjecting himself to alcohol and opium

CHARLOTTE BRONTË

abuse for many years, and he died in 1848 – officially from tuberculosis, now thought to have been brought on by his drug and drink habits. He was just thirty-one years old.

At the same time, Anne and Emily both became ill with tuberculosis. Emily died in December 1848, aged thirty.

Charlotte took Anne (who was now her only sibling) to Scarborough in May 1849, hoping that the sea air would help to cure her. Unfortunately, Anne died just four days after their arrival, aged only twenty-nine. She was buried in Scarborough so that their father didn't have to suffer the pain of yet another family funeral.

Shortly afterwards, Charlotte wrote:

> "A year ago – had a prophet warned me how I should stand in June 1849 – how stripped and bereaved....I should have thought – this can never be endured..."

Charlotte turned to her writing for comfort in these bleak times, and her next novel, *Shirley,* was published in October 1849.

She was now quite famous and attracted a great deal of attention. For instance, during one of her many visits to London she not only met her literary idol, W.M.Thackeray, but she also had her portrait painted by popular High Society artist George Richmond.

Her next novel, *Villette,* published in 1853, was to be her last.

During this time, Charlotte had also attracted the personal attention of her father's curate, the Reverend Arthur Bell Nicholls. Charlotte initially rejected Reverend Nicholls' proposal for marriage, probably due to her father thinking that Nicholls was not worthy of his now-famous daughter. Eventually, however, her father softened, and Charlotte married Reverend Nicholls in Haworth Church on 29, June 1854, and the couple spent their honeymoon in Ireland. Once again, this is mirrored in *Jane Eyre*, in which Jane attracts the interest of a religious man, and in which Mr. Rochester suggests sending her away to Ireland. More interestingly, however, these actual events took place after *Jane Eyre* was written!

Charlotte became pregnant, and at the same time, her health began to decline. Elizabeth Gaskell, Charlotte's earliest biographer, writes that she was attacked by "sensations of perpetual nausea and ever-recurring faintness."

Charlotte and her unborn child died on March 31, 1855, three weeks before her thirty-ninth birthday. Her death certificate gives the cause of death as phthisis (tuberculosis).

Her husband, Reverend Nicholls, looked after Charlotte's father, Patrick, for six years until Patrick's death in June 1861 at the age of eighty-four.

Other than Patrick, none of the Brontës of Haworth enjoyed a long life, and none of them had any children to carry on the literary name.

"Gentle, soft dream, nestling in my arms now, you will fly, too, as your sisters have all fled before you:"

(from Jane Eyre, *written while her younger sisters were alive).*

THE BRONTË FAMILY TREE

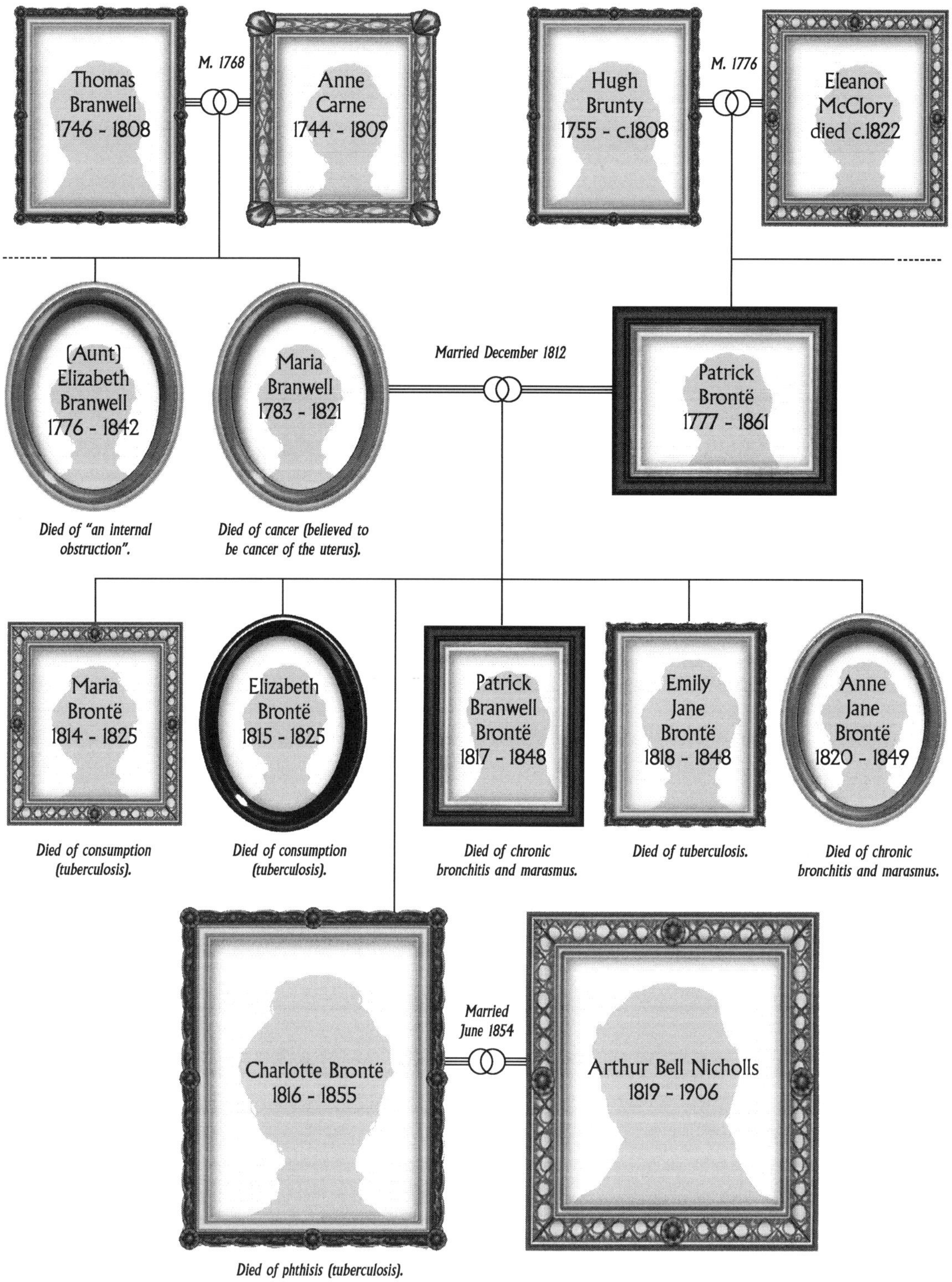

Key:
Parent of ————
Married ═○○═

Due to the lack of official records of births, deaths and marriages within this period, the above information is derived from extensive research and is as accurate as possible from the limited sources available.

CHARLOTTE BRONTË - TRUE OR FALSE?

TRUE OR FALSE?	ANSWER:
Charlotte's father was a teacher in Yorkshire.	
Charlotte was an only child.	
Charlotte lived for most of her life in Brussels, Belgium.	
Her first book was *Persuasion.*	
Brontë wasn't the family's real name.	
There is a museum dedicated to the Brontës.	
Charlotte was first married when she was eighteen.	
Charlotte used the pen name Currer Bell.	
Charlotte's middle name was Jane.	
Charlotte died when she was seventy years old.	

CHARLOTTE BRONTË – RESEARCH TEMPLATE

QUESTION:	ANSWER:
Where and when was Charlotte Brontë born?	
Whom did she marry?	
What was the name of her first novel? (Written, not published.)	
What was the name of her second novel?	
Where did Charlotte live in February 1842?	
How much did Charlotte and her siblings pay to have *Poems* published?	
How many copies did they sell in the first year?	
Who published Charlotte's biography in 1857?	
When was her novel *The Professor* first published?	
In which novel would you find Shirley Keeldar?	
Name all of Charlotte's novels.	
Name Charlotte's siblings.	

THE BRONTËS – A CHRONOLOGY

1816 **April 21**: Charlotte is born at Thornton, the third daughter of Patrick Brontë and Maria Branwell Brontë.

1817 **June 26**: Patrick Branwell Brontë is born.

1818 **July 30**: Emily Jane Brontë is born.

1820 **January 17**: Anne Brontë is born.
February: Patrick ,Sr. is appointed curate at Haworth.
April: the Brontë family moves to Haworth.

1821 **September**: Maria Brontë dies of cancer. Her sister, Elizabeth Branwell, moves in with the family.

1824 **July**: Elizabeth and Maria are sent to the Clergy Daughters' School at Cowan Bridge, Lancashire.
August: Charlotte and Emily are also sent to the Clergy Daughters' School (the school became a model for Lowood School in *Jane Eyre*).

1825 Elizabeth and Maria both return home from school in ill health. Maria dies in **May** and Elizabeth dies in **June** (both from tuberculosis, or "consumption"). Charlotte and Emily are removed from the school and sent home.

1826-1831 To entertain themselves, the children fill the pages of miniature homemade books with stories about imaginary kingdoms, inspired by some toy soldiers given to Branwell as a gift.

1831 **January**: Charlotte attends Miss Wooler's school at Roe Head, Mirfield. Here she meets lifelong friends Mary Taylor and Ellen Nussey.

1832 **June**: Charlotte leaves Roe Head to return home and teach her sisters.

1835 **July**: Charlotte returns to Roe Head as a teacher, taking Emily with her as a free pupil.
October: Emily returns home, and Anne takes her place.

1838 **December**: Charlotte resigns her position and returns to Haworth.

1839 **March**: Charlotte rejects a marriage proposal from Reverend Henry Nussey, Ellen's brother.
May to **July**: Charlotte works as a governess in Lothersdale.
July: Charlotte rejects another marriage proposal, this time from Mr. Pryce – an Irish curate.

1841 Charlotte works as a governess at Rawdon from **March** to **December**.

1842 **February**: Charlotte and Emily go to Brussels to study languages at the Pensionnat Heger.
October: Their aunt Elizabeth dies.
November: Charlotte and Emily return to Haworth.

1843 **January**: Charlotte returns to Brussels alone but is lonely and becomes depressed. She forms an attachment to Constantin Heger, the head of the school, whose intellect appeals to her. Madame Heger's jealousy necessitates Charlotte's departure.

1844 With all of the siblings now back at Haworth, the family tries to start a school at the Haworth parsonage, but it is not a success.

1845 The Reverend Arthur Bell Nicholls becomes curate at Haworth.

1846 **April**: Charlotte, Emily, and Anne publish at their own expense a joint volume of *Poems* by Currer, Ellis, and Acton Bell. Only two copies are sold. Charlotte's novel *The Professor* is rejected by publishers.
August: Charlotte begins *Jane Eyre* while caring for her father, who is recovering from an eye operation.

1847 **October**: *Jane Eyre* is published and is an immediate success. It starts off life as *Jane Eyre: An Autobiography* Edited by Currer Bell as if Jane Eyre was a real person and Charlotte Brontë, working under her assumed name of Currer Bell, was merely the editor.

1848 **September**: Charlotte starts *Shirley*; Branwell dies of tuberculosis.
December: Emily dies of tuberculosis. Anne also becomes ill.

1849 **May**: Charlotte tries to nurse Anne back to health and takes her to Scarborough. She dies four days after they arrive there.
October: *Shirley - A Tale by Currer Bell* is published.

1849-1851 Charlotte travels frequently. She is invited to London as the guest of her publisher, where she meets Thackeray.
She also visits the Lake District, Scotland, and Manchester, where she meets with Elizabeth Gaskell, her future biographer.

1851 **April**: She rejects a marriage proposal from James Taylor, a member of her publishing house.

1853 **January**: *Villette*, a novel set in Brussels, is published, still by Currer Bell.

1854 **June**: Charlotte marries her suitor Arthur Bell Nichols, her father's curate. She begins but does not finish a novel, *Emma*.

1855 **March**: Charlotte dies during her pregnancy and is buried at The Parsonage at Haworth.

1857 **March**: Elizabeth Gaskell's *The Life of Charlotte Brontë* is published.
June: Her previously rejected novel *The Professor* is published posthumously.

OVERVIEW OF THE PERIOD

Date	What was happening in life and literature
1792	Mary Wollstonecraft publishes her *Vindication of the Rights of Women.*
1807	*Slave Trade Abolition Bill* passes in the British Parliament.
1811	First Luddite riot. George, Prince of Wales becomes the Prince Regent because his father, George III, is believed to be insane (the Regency Acts of 1811).
1813	Jane Austen publishes *Pride and Prejudice.*
1815	Napoleon returns from exile for 100 days – is defeated at Waterloo.
1816	Jane Austen publishes *Emma.* Mary Shelley (daughter of Mary Wollstonecraft) writes *Frankenstein.*
1817	Death of Jane Austen. Bill raised to abolish the public whipping of women.
1820	Death of George III (end of the Regency). George IV accedes and tries to dissolve his marriage with Caroline.
1821	The poet John Keats dies.
1824	Death of Byron.
1825	First railway, Stockton to Darlington, Yorkshire is completed.
1829	Catholic Emancipation.
1830	George IV dies. William IV accedes.
1831	Cholera epidemic in the UK.
1832	First (Or Great) *Reform Act* passes. Anna Jameson publishes *Characteristics of Women.* Death of Walter Scott and Goethe.
1836	Charles Dickens *Pickwick Papers* first published as a serial.
1838	*The People's Charter* drafted. Chartist movement is born.
1839	Charter rejected by Parliament. Riots in Birmingham, England.
1840	Death of Fanny Burney (novelist).
1842	2nd Chartist petition – rejected.
1843	Margaret Fuller publishes *The Great Lawsuit – Man versus Men, Woman versus Women.*
1845	Irish potato famine. Margaret Fuller publishes *Women In the Nineteenth Century.*
1846	Repeal of the Corn Laws.
1847	William Thackeray: serialisation of *Vanity Fair* begins.
1848	Final Chartist petition – rejected. Revolutions in Paris, Berlin, Vienna, Venice, Prague, Budapest. Marx and Engels publish the *Communist Manifesto.* Elizabeth Gaskell publishes her first novel, *Mary Barton.*
1849	Cholera epidemic. *Eliza Cook's Journal* begins.
1851	The Great Exhibition (Crystal Palace). Harriet Taylor publishes *Enfranchisement of Women.*
1852	Harriet Beecher Stowe publishes *Uncle Tom's Cabin.*
1854	Yet another cholera epidemic!

YOU COULDN'T MAKE IT UP!

Charlotte was born into a world where it was still legal to whip women. The British government finally completely abolished this practice in 1820, the year Charlotte's youngest sister Anne was born. That is less than 200 years ago!

Jane Eyre is the autobiography of Jane Eyre, not Charlotte Brontë (and even the fictional character "Jane" describes her autobiography as a novel on two occasions). Brontë said the only similarity between her and her heroine was her physical looks – little and plain. It is always a mistake to read a novel *as if it is a biography* of the author. It's better to "read" a person's life as its own vast sprawling narrative running alongside and in and out of countless other narratives. Every time we read the history of Charlotte's *life*, let alone her novels, we will see different things in it (for example, the "Creole" Bertha gets more sympathy these days than she did from Victorian readers). Nothing is permanent. But it IS important to know that Charlotte is not "making it up" in the sense that she is not saying things about society that just weren't true.

For example, Lowood School is not the Cowan Bridge School for the daughters of clergymen that Charlotte really attended, just given a different name. Nor is Thornfield really Norton Conyers near Ripon, North Yorkshire, though the tourist board and heritage industry there might be happy for you to think so. Both are narratives and places in the life of a woman called Charlotte Brontë who later used some key aspects of both to create a fiction with its own links and purposes, a period in the life – a pattern in the psychological development – of a *made up* character. Nevertheless, Victorian children did die of epidemic diseases in appallingly run schools. Similarly, governesses often worked in places like Thornfield, in precarious moral circumstances, caught between their status as ladies and their life as servants.

Charlotte is not, at least in this, writing a fairy story. She is using real life for her own purposes, and (as with Dickens) one of those purposes is to draw attention to what is wrong with society, for the poor, for orphans, for women, for children. And the real life of this real society is often shocking by modern standards. In this respect, it is important to know what the actual "condition of women" – in education, as governesses, and in terms of religious orthodoxy – was in the Brontës' age.

TASK 1:

Compare *Jane Eyre* to Charlotte's own life story (Use the Brontë time line on page 14 and the synopsis of the novel, starting on page 28, to help you. You'll be able to find out more in books or on the Internet). Find THREE major events in her life story that don't occur in the novel and vice versa. Find THREE events that happened in both. (Caution – this could be partly a trick question).

TASK 2:

What were the Luddite riots about?
How did they start?
When and why did they end?

TASK 3:

What was *The People's Charter*? Describe events from the first draft to the final rejection.

EMANCIPATION AND DISCONTENT

Charlotte Brontë lived in an age both like and very unlike our own. She grew up in a large family of five sisters and one brother, all deprived of their mother at an early age (their mother died of cancer when Charlotte was five) and with an aunt replacing their mother. The four elder girls were sent away to a boarding school for clergymen's daughters. Charlotte's two elder sisters died of tuberculosis there before reaching their teens. The unhealthy conditions and poor diet at the school as well as the general poverty of its students would leave the pupils weak and vulnerable to the disease. The lack of a cure for TB and of effective anti-epidemic measures in those times exacerbated the problem. Charlotte and Emily were sent home and recovered, but many girls at the school didn't.

The differences with our own age start to become clear.

Charlotte's other sisters survived childhood but were both dead before they reached thirty, Emily of TB. Her only brother might have enjoyed better health (and education) like his father, but he killed himself with alcohol abuse at thirty-one. Later, her father became very ill and nearly blind, and Charlotte had to interrupt a teaching career in Brussels in her late 20s to come home and nurse him. Some of this is still very unlike our own time, some more familiar.

Few modern girls would receive a marriage proposal from three different clergymen as Charlotte did, though. She rejected all three, changing her mind and finally accepting the third, her father's curate Arthur Bell Nichols, and marrying him in 1854. As a young girl in Brussels, she was possibly in love with an older man, Constantin Heger, one of her employers at the Pensionnat Heger. Having finally married her third clergyman, Charlotte succumbed to TB and pneumonia during pregnancy and died in 1855, just weeks before her 39th birthday, not an advanced age, but still ten years after her siblings had died.

This catalog of literally murderous schooling, fatal tuberculosis and constant bereavement and struggle is by no means untypical of Charlotte's age – Victorian families were large, their health was fragile and the environment was one of the unhealthiest and polluted in history. Mortality was frequent – but it may appear like a horror story to modern eyes. What is unusual in *any* time is that all three of the Brontë sisters who survived into adulthood became famous novelists, though only Charlotte lived long enough to experience fame fully. All three are still read, and at least two are usually considered to be geniuses. In this respect, Charlotte's family background is exceptional in any age: not many of us grow up with two geniuses across the breakfast table (or, for that matter, any at all).

Discontent

In *Jane Eyre*, Charlotte's narrator defends herself against any accusation of being a "discontent." The novel was written and published in an age of great discontent; read more about Luddites and Charterists to see why. Despite the convention that little children should be seen and not heard, many Victorian novelists, poets and thinkers used images of rebellious yet "imprisoned" children as an illustration of or allegory for their rebellion against the society that oppresses them.

EMANCIPATION AND DISCONTENT

Wuthering Heights includes an early passage where its hero and heroine, Heathcliff and Catherine, rebel together against unjust punishment as children, very like Jane in the Red Room. Both passages have been read as a symbol of the spirit of rebellion against oppression. The first readers of *Jane Eyre* in the late 1840s read the story with political disturbances in the air at home (the Chartists) and violent revolutions all over Europe. Charlotte was accused of being a troublemaker just like such political activists, stirring up discontent. Her heroine should have been more ladylike, said influential critics, more quiet and passive in the face of all hardship and disappointment. The longings for a better and wider life she feels at every stage – in the confines of the red room, in the narrowness of her assistant teacher life after Miss Temple's departure from Lowood, as a dutiful but bored governess on the battlements at Thornfield, in the prospect of being a missionary's wife (going to wider horizons but only in rigid confinement to St. John) – are all active rebellions against what a Victorian girl and lady *should* want. *Jane Eyre* is a very bold statement – one of the first – of what a woman really does want. Passionate fulfilment. Love. Active self-expression. Freedom.

She may call Rochester her "master," and the idea of love as a voluntary submission (in marriage) to another is strong throughout. But subordination is not at all conveyed by the final chapter's "Reader, I married him."

The way that Jane's own story of confinement and escape is paralleled by Bertha's – her bedroom at Thornfield is right under Bertha's attic prison, and Jane's "mad cat" fixed chair in the red room is exactly Bertha's situation – can be read two ways.
Either Jane as a mature, grown-up woman must learn to stop behaving like a "mad cat" child through self-control, or she will end up like Bertha. But Bertha and Jane have more in common than a casual reader might think: Bertha is perhaps a copy of Jane's most rebellious self. Either way, the "discontents" of this (female) protagonist in an age that both violently repressed and gradually emancipated masses of people reflects the widespread discontents of its time.

TASK 1:

Imagine that you are Bertha, trapped in a strange land at the mercy of a man who no longer loves you, locked in an attic room in a remote country house, friendless, penniless and helpless.

a) Write a warning letter to Jane based on your experience of marriage to Rochester.
b) Plan your escape from the house in as much detail as you can imagine. What would you need? Where would you go? Who could you rely on?

TASK 2:

Why was childhood mortality so high in Charlotte's lifetime?
There are a number of reasons, so research carefully, giving at least three reasons – not just a list of diseases either!

THE POSITION OF VICTORIAN WOMEN

The position of a woman in the Victorian society Brontë lived and wrote in was very different from now. She was legally, socially, politically, economically, religiously, physically, educationally and – in the way she was perceived – intellectually and artistically inferior to men. (Average weight of Man's Brain 3½ lbs, Woman's 2lbs 11oz was a popular "scientific" proof.) But in one crucial way, she was in a much better position than in previous ages. "The Woman Question" – the debate about gender – was a key issue. "The greatest social difficulty in England today is the relationship between men and women," wrote Justin McCarthy in an essay on novels in 1864. And Charlotte Brontë was one of many women who contributed to this debate. "The author is very bitter against *men*...the social position of women is not at all what it should be, and hence she speaks in her angry and indignant tone," wrote one reviewer of Charlotte's novel *Shirley* (1849). In the novel, a woman is so bored with her life living in her clergyman uncle's house, with no outlet for her intelligence and passions, that she wishes for death. It was the experience of many middle-class Victorian women, as Jane Eyre says in the earlier novel.

"Women are supposed to be very calm generally: but women feel just as men feel; they need exercise for their faculties and a field for their efforts as much as their brothers do... it is narrow minded to say... they ought to confine themselves to making puddings and knitting stockings, to playing on the piano and embroidering bags."

By 1873, George Meredith was even declaring that the test of a civilization is whether men "consent to talk on equal terms with women, and listen to them". (*Essay on Comedy*). There was definite progress in at least drawing attention to the existence of women – and their potential rights – in the Victorian period. Examples included not just intellectual, upper- and middle-class women like Florence Nightingale, who cut loose from family constraints to carve a career, or the impoverished orphans of the gentry who became governesses (like Jane) whom Brontë typically champions, but working-class women, too. Over a quarter of the nation's women had jobs, often in low-paid toil as domestics, seamstresses, factory workers, miners and farm labourers, and in 1888, the "Match Girls," supported by the radical organizer Annie Besant, became the first union – after many male union defeats – to win a strike for higher wages and the abolition of work fines. It has often been the way in English history.

In Tudor times, one of the most patriarchal periods in history, Mary I became the first reigning English queen, and she was swiftly followed by Elizabeth I, whose reign was the longest until that of Victoria. Prostitutes began to publish their eloquent stories in *The Times* in 1858, drawing attention – and the attention of politicians and social reformers like Charles Dickens and William Gladstone (later the long-serving Prime Minister) – to their plight. As one prostitute wrote, "If I am hideous cancer in society, are not the causes of the disease to be found in the rottenness of the carcass?"

So the very real Victorian oppression of women, including their inability to vote, own property or win custody of her own children, has to be seen in perspective. The oppression itself had gone on for centuries: Victorian women, radicals and progressive men merely drew attention to it and slowly began to address it.

Not all agreed with such progressive thinking. Sarah Ellis's bestseller of 1839, *The Women of England,* published sixteen editions in two years! It became the basis of her school for girls – a school which avoided intellectual subjects in favor of training the emotions – and venerated the female as the husband's help at work in times of trouble and trial –

THE POSITION OF VICTORIAN WOMEN

"a humble monitress who sat alone, guarding the fireside comforts of his distant home" and "sent him back to that beloved home, a wiser and a better man." This faithful, supportive wife of missionary William Ellis (they married in 1837) wrote, "The long established customs of [England] have placed in [women's] hands the high and holy duty of cherishing and protecting the minor morals of life, from whence springs all that elevated in purpose, and glorious in action." "All the heroines, whether of romance and reality [have not been] the learned, the accomplished women, the women who could solve problems, and elucidate systems of philosophy? No ... they have been women dignified with moral greatness. ... What man is there in existence who would not rather his wife should be free from selfishness, than be able to read Virgil without the use of a [Latin] dictionary."

Charlotte might answer that Virgil teaches just such a freedom from selfishness and that her heroine Jane was both a heroine of moral greatness like this – setting an example that saved both Rochester and herself from repeating his earlier mistakes – and a real woman with thoughts, feelings and temptations of her own. And that the brilliant Brontës, like Jane Austen before and Harriet Martineau (1802–1876) after her, would be supposed (because they were women) to "cover up [their] manuscripts with a large piece of muslin work, kept on the table for the purpose, whenever any genteel people came in". (Or, in their case, hide them under the pseudonyms Acton, Currer and Bell.) And Virginia Woolf would assert that the sentimental title of "angel in the house" not only disguises that the man not only owns and controls that house but that women are patronized and oppressed by being placed on a pedestal: they cannot then be themselves.

But such moral and emotional wifely support for husbands was not invented by the Victorians; it was merely identified and valued by them. Victoria herself, while forbidding her prime ministers Gladstone and Disraeli to introduce any form of voting rights for women ("this mad folly") embodied such a role and enthroned it, at the most visible public level. Her devotion to her husband made highly visible a supporting role that earlier societies had taken for granted or even been blind to. She was the very large angel in the royal house as her potent support for the founding of a woman's college in 1847 made even clearer. If part of the oppressiveness of domesticity is that it is unseen, the Victorians put the subjection and service of women center stage.

The winds of change blew only fitfully, and they finally began to prevail from about 1970. (Interestingly, the "angel in the house" was sent from the hearth by the Government in the 1940s, when the country needed active independent women to keep the country and the home front running, while the men won the war. In the 1960s young men began the rebellion against women trying to tie them down – *Saturday Night and Sunday Morning*, the Who, Hendrix – and women empowered by the Pill took up the fight for equality as the 1960s became the 1970s.) The debate goes on, but Charlotte was one of the first women to contribute to that debate, and her views remain surprisingly advanced and modern.

Employment and women

Charlotte presents Jane Eyre as an independent woman, keen on the rights and vocal about the undervalued skills and talents of her sex. Jane comments pointedly on women's lack of independence and the subservient position she has in society. The difficulties she has in making a living reflect the knowledge and experience her creator Brontë had in attempting to do just that. As Jane Austen knew, it was not respectable for a "lady" to earn her own living. One could work of course, but not for vulgar pay. This included middle-class women like the Brontës, though it should be remembered that working class women (and girls) could toil in the mines and mills without comment. A "lady" was expected to make a career out of marriage or charity work. If a young middle-class woman like Jane wanted to support herself without losing her reputation or her class status, there was only one available career, that of a governess, too poor to be a real lady but too middle-class to be a worker, caught somewhere between a lady and a servant. A respectable servitude.

THE POSITION OF VICTORIAN WOMEN

It is arguable whether women have achieved real – as opposed to the principle of – equality with men even in our own time. The problems of balancing families with careers and the many enduring prejudices of a patriarchal heritage still inhibit women's equal progress in the workplace. But compared to Charlotte's world, women have progressed economically, socially, legally, educationally and personally beyond all but the wildest dreams of 1847.

1832 Reform Act

Like all women of her time, Charlotte could not vote. (Women in the UK would not get the vote until 1918, and young women not until 1928). Most men could not vote either – though this began to change in Charlotte's lifetime with the *1832 Reform Act*. But the idea of women achieving enfranchisement and equality of various kinds – remote though the reality seemed – was a growing feature of the Victorian period. It began in the political unrest of an earlier period, coming out of the French and American Revolutions and with Mary Wollstonecraft's pioneering (and at the time pie in the sky) book *Vindication of the Rights of Woman* in 1792. But Charlotte would certainly never be able to vote in her lifetime. She would also lose the rights to her own property on marriage. (This law was finally abolished in 1888.) It is argued that women did not even have the legal ownership of their own bodies. For example, until 1864 a man had the power to take a women to court if she did not grant him his "conjugal rights." She would also have had very limited educational options.

Charlotte understood the problem through her own experience as a teacher, a governess, and a struggling writer. The character she chooses to represent such young women and their problems – Jane Eyre – therefore has a considerable basis in her own life and adds a personal sadness to the portrait. Jane Eyre is also a carefully researched and constructed character. There were many books and articles published on the subject of "the condition of Woman Question" in the 1840s, and Charlotte read them avidly. The subject was of profound importance to her.

The male – female divide

The males of rich families were typically sent away to boarding schools, as John Reed was. The secondary education of girls was almost non-existent. It was believed that girls did not have the intellectual capacity to benefit from it and would not need schooling for their future lives. Ladies – upper- and middle-class women – were trained in certain "accomplishments," like embroidery, singing, painting and playing the piano, as adornments to their married lives. Young ladies of little fortune like Jane Eyre would need to know a foreign language and have enough of an elementary education to work as governesses, and schools like Lowood existed to provide this.

THE POSITION OF VICTORIAN WOMEN

Poorer girls toiled from a very early age at housework and/or – like their male counterparts – at work in the mills and mines. Hannah is an example of this servant class, as are Miss Abbot and Bessie. As an orphan, Jane begins her life at a lower level than a servant. “Am I a servant?” “No, you are less than a servant for you do nothing for your keep.” Part of the novel’s journey is how Jane changes from this orphan of no status to asserting her position as a lady. The cottage girls Jane teaches show a new Victorian concern for literacy to be spread to the working classes and to give them the skills needed in the new kind of industrial society Britain was becoming.

***Jane Eyre* reflecting the age.**

The whole novel of *Jane Eyre* is preoccupied with the theme of education and the function it has in expanding a person’s horizons. Jane is a stern but fair teacher, disliking Lowood’s cruelties but also wary of the indulgence of children along what she calls “French” lines. She is as successful and conscientious a teacher in St. John’s school at Morton as she is a governess, and she moves Adèle around several schools before she is satisfied with the type and standard of education.

One of the themes of *Jane Eyre* is the prejudice against girls and women in terms of intellect and capacity for thought. It was devoutly believed – and had been throughout the Middle Ages – that women were inferior in terms of intelligence whereas in fact they were simply less educated. As girls were admitted into further education, their success at all levels – including the very highest university level in terms of the “blue ribbon” prizes – put paid to the long prejudices against them. The impact of previously untapped female intelligence in subsequent human progress and research is self-evident. Perhaps even more significant is the improvement in female lives and fulfilment, a key theme of *Jane Eyre*. And – another key theme – the enrichment of the male-female relationship founded on equality.

The education of girls was a key issue in 1847 and throughout the period. The legacy was for “young ladies” to be moulded by – and for – eighteenth century “manners.”

But as the nineteenth century progressed, the Victorians of Charlotte’s own period added a strong moral element to this. The combination of eighteenth century manners and Victorian respectability in education was not good news for self-expression, as Jane’s conflict with Mr. Brocklehurst shows. (Brocklehurst believes girls should be children of “grace,” not “nature” – and this means that even a naturally curly haired girl should somehow repress her curls.) Female personality was not expressed by education. It was *repressed* by it.

Education and religion

This had a lot to do with Victorian religion. Although without religion there would have been no schools for the girls in the book at all (as Brocklehurst and St. John both show), there was a high price to pay for it. Victorian Christianity – especially the “progressive” type that cared about education for all – was very strict.

If the generalization is that eighteenth-century men preferred their women dependent and frail and nineteenth century men preferred them ignorant, it is also that the men of both centuries insisted that women were “good.” And in Victorian Britain, goodness meant charity and service. So the education of girls involved a lot of training in how to serve others.

THE POSITION OF VICTORIAN WOMEN

Traditional roles of caring for children and the sick became a more scientific training in nursing and (elementary) teaching – and (eventually) training as doctors and higher grades of teaching. The right to vote, graduate and dispose of one's own property after marriage were all Victorian concerns. And they are all really about a woman being herself, an individual, which is the key theme of *Jane Eyre*. Jane Eyre is deliberately not the traditional pretty, isolated heroine of earlier books – she is a plain woman just trying to be herself. And part of that is that her intelligence is not even defined or limited by her gender. She is certainly a passionate woman, but she is also a human being, at least an equal with Rochester. Queen Victoria opposed votes for women and most of the feminism of the new woman. But the long period she gave her name to marks a watershed in female self-definition. And the education of girls was a key element of this.

Victorian Education was both a moral education and a practical one. Even in the eighteenth century writers like Swift were demanding a "better" sort of woman. But the curriculum a girl received was driven by the role she might play. A girl was always a prospective wife – whether of a gentleman or a factory hand. Unless she became a nun (less common than in the middle ages but still an option, as Eliza shows) marriage was the assumed career destination of girls. Their teachers assumed it. Some girls – especially among those with enough of their own money not to wish to lose it to their husbands – did not marry. Most unmarried girls subsisted on a "small annuity" and/or worked as "companions" or servants in houses or shops.

Public education for girls, therefore, usually meant a grounding in morals and behavior to last all through her life, perhaps including a superficial layer of "accomplishments" to pass the time, help attract a man or – if things got really bad, as they do for Jane – to earn a living. More homes in Victorian times provided intelligent girls with books, travel, conversation and encouragement than before, but this was a private and accidental provision, not part of a national curriculum. It depended on the luck of having a wise mother, a sympathetic father with a good home library, or an enlightened husband – and it was generally a middle- and upper-class luck even then.

After Tennyson's 1847 publication of *The Princess*, which highlights issues of "the education of the poor man before making him our master, and the higher education of women," Victorians saw the establishment of Queen's College – an institute that opened in 1848 with the express purpose of educating young women, including would-be governesses; King's College undertook to train governesses, and Bedford College started with classes held in a private house. By the 1850s, and despite very slow progress, the higher education of women had at least begun. In April 1850 Frances Mary Buss opened the North London Collegiate School for Ladies at 46 Camden Street. In 1854 Cheltenham Ladies College was created and went from strength to strength under the leadership of Miss Beale. She was to devote the next forty-eight years to the development of the college, which at the time of her death in 1906 had grown to a community of some one thousand pupils.

TASK 1:

Produce a timeline showing landmarks in the suffrage movement from the 17th to the 20th century.

TASK 2:

Show on the timeline landmark achievements for women, first published female author, first registered doctor, pilot, graduate, etc.

TIMELINE OF LEGAL, ECONOMIC AND SOCIAL RIGHTS LEGISLATION FOR WOMEN

1820 It is made illegal to whip women.

1832 *Reform Act* (and then the *1835 Municipal Corporations Act*) formally prohibit women from voting.

1833 *Factory Act*. Children under thirteen limited to nine hours labor per day.

1838 Chartism has large and active female membership. No subsequent suffrage movement mentions women at all until much later. The Chartists support the rights of women only in the context of the continued rights of husbands over wives (most members were husbands with wives); they were not feminists. But this superbly organized independent working-class organization – a model for many that followed – sows the seeds of later enfranchisement.

1839 Sarah Ellis publishes her best seller *The Women of England*. It recommends the education of women solely for their domestic role as the "heart" of a marriage, a living daily example to her returning husband of the "disinterested kindness" and "unselfishness" so absent from the ruthless and competitive world of Victorian capitalism.

1842 Report of the Children's Employment Commission 1842 includes a picture of a girl "hurrying" coal along a narrow underground tunnel in the Halifax district. She is on all fours, half naked and drawing a coal trolley filled with between two to five hundred pounds like a horse.

1844 Factory Bill classes women as young persons. (Tory) *Factory Act* – to limit the exploitation of women by factory owners, women's working day is restricted to a maximum of twelve hours, (between 5.30am and 8.30pm – to help inspectors monitor). All machinery must be fenced, and no woman (or child) may clean a moving machine. Women's clothes were particularly apt to get caught in the machinery, and a girl in Stockport had been carried by her clothing round an upright shaft – her thighs broken and ankles dislocated.

1847 (Whig) *Factory Act* – women's working day is restricted to ten hours. Tennyson publishes *The Princess*, a serious discussion of the education of women, to huge public interest. *Jane Eyre* by "Currer Bell" published.

1848 More radically than even the European martyrs of 1848, the Chartists demand universal adult suffrage and only substitute universal male suffrage on the grounds of immediate feasibility. Queen's College, London opens, aims to provide university education for women. Bedford College, London, follows.

1850 Miss Buss founds The North London Collegiate School (for girls).

1856 Florence Nightingale is granted £50,000 to train nurses at St. Thomas and King's College Hospitals. No medical training for women was previously available. (She herself trained in religious houses in Europe.)

1857 *Divorce Act*. Simplified existing divorce laws to this: Men could divorce women if they were adulterous once (because of the chance of rogue bastards spoiling inheritance and family lineage). Women could only divorce men after "repeated and aggravated infidelity".

1858 Florence Nightingale *Notes on Nursing* – helps reform army hospitals.

1864 Schools' Enquiry Commission includes girls' schools in its purview. University of Cambridge petitioned to open entry examinations to girls.

1865 It is recognized that universities have duties concerning the education of women.

1869 Women win the right to vote in municipal elections. University extension movement helps create two women's colleges at Cambridge: Girton (1869) and Newnham (1871). The monastic tradition of education finally challenged.

1870 Women win the right to vote in elections to the local boards to oversee the new elementary schools.

1871 A Society for Promoting the Employment of Women is in existence. Miss Beale (Cheltenham College) asks, "Why should it be thought dishonourable for a woman to earn money?" The typewriter (like factory machinery earlier) provides a new occupation in business at which women's nimble hands are usually more skilful than men's. The bicycle liberates young ladies from the need to be escorted outside the home by father or brother.

1872 National Society for Women's Suffrage formed (NSWS).

1874 The Girls Public Day School Trust formed – establishes schools in London, Manchester, Portsmouth and other cities.

1878 *Matrimonial Causes Act.* Allows women to divorce and take children into their custody if their husbands have been convicted of assaulting them. London University opens its examinations and degrees to women.

1881 Women at Newnham and Girton may now take honors courses, though not receive degrees.

1882 – (and **1893**) *Married Women's Property Acts.* Married women no longer relinquish their property to their husbands.

1884 *Married Women's Property Act* [Amendment]. Recognizes women as an independent and separate person within marriage, no longer a chattel belonging to the husband.

1884 Abolition of imprisonment for woman refusing conjugal rights to husband.

1885 "Lawn Tennis has taught women how much they are capable of doing" (*The Field* magazine). Athletics still difficult because of clothing.

1886 *Guardianship and Custody of Infants Act.* Women could be sole guardian of their children if their husbands die. (Minor and ongoing improvements concerning the legal position of deserted wives or widows of intestate husbands.)

1888 Match Girls Union – unusual then for unskilled workers to have a union – formed to demand higher wages and end "White slavery in London." Wins strike, the first trade union strike victory ever.

1892 The four Scottish universities and their degrees now completely open to women. Durham follows suit in 1895.

1893 Women can vote in New Zealand.

1897 National Union of Women's Suffrage Societies (NUWSS) splits from NSWS.

1902 Russell Bill. Tries to widen legal grounds for divorce.

1902 Women can vote in Australia.

1903 Women's Social and Political Union splinters from NSWS and begins militant action.

1903 Trinity College Dublin opens its classes, degrees and prizes to women and confers ad eundem degrees on women holding degree certificates from Oxbridge. All the newly founded Universities in England, Wales and Ireland admit women on equal terms with men.

1906 Women can vote in Finland.

1907 Women can stand in elections.

1908 Suffragettes try to storm the Houses of Parliament. Olympics held in London, women are allowed to compete.

1909 First suffragette hunger strike in prison. Marion Wallace Dunlop released after ninety-one hours.

1909–1912 Gorell Commission. Royal report recommends that women be granted equal rights to those of men in matters of divorce. Not implemented.

1918 *Representation of the People Act.* Women over the age of thirty who are householders, the wives of householders, occupiers of property with an annual rent of £5 or graduates of British universities can vote. Votes for "respectable" women aged thirty and over! Constance Markiewicz was elected for the constituency of Dublin St. Patrick's as one of seventy-three Sinn Fein MPs. This made her the first woman elected to the British House of Commons. (However, in line with Sinn Féin policy, she refused to take her seat.)

1919 *Sex Disqualification Removal Act* (allows election of women to municipal committees).

1920 Women can vote in the US.

1921 Oxford University opens its degrees, prizes and scholarships to women (Cambridge still does not).

1924 A service drawn up in the Anglican prayer book for the ordination of deaconesses – later removed (except in China).

1925 *Separation and Maintenance Act.*

1926 Universities Commission makes it possible for women to work as university lecturers. Cambridge women may now receive degrees and prizes.
Widows & Pensions Act.

1928 *Equal Franchise Act.* All adults over the age of twenty-one, except lunatics, criminals and members of the House of Lords, given the right to vote. Universal Suffrage!

1929 Virginia Woolf publishes *A Room Of One's Own*, a dissertation on the artificial stunting of female potential in patriarchal society.

1937 *Matrimonial Causes Act.* Implements the recommendations of the Gorell Commission. Women permitted to apply for divorce on grounds of unlawful desertion for two years or more, cruelty, or incurable insanity on the part of their husbands.

1944 Women can vote in France.

1993 Priests (Ordination of Women) Measure passed. Women in the established church of England may be ordained as priests. ("Vicars in knickers" is *The Sun's* headline.)

THE POSITION OF VICTORIAN WOMEN

TASK 1:
Show on a map of the world which countries were the 1st, 2nd, 3rd and so on to allow all adults to vote.

TASK 2:
Do the same exercise showing votes for women.

TASK 3:
Education was an issue for the poor too. Research education in Victorian times, and find answers to the following:

Who funded schools In the Victorian era?
Did working children receive any education at all?
Did standards differ between rural and urban communities?

When were education acts passed, making schooling compulsory?
What are the legal requirements today?
Who funds education now?

TEST YOURSELF

1. **Which country gave the vote to women first? France, Finland or England?**
2. **When did the *Representation of the People Act* come into being?**
3. **When could women first stand in elections in the UK?**
4. **Which country was the first (of currently independent countries) to give the vote to women?**
5. **Who began training for nurses in 1856?**
6. **Who wrote *The Princess*?**
7. **Which bestseller of 1839 did Sarah Ellis write?**
8. **Mary Wollstonecraft is the famous mother of which writer?**
9. **When was *The People's Charter* first drafted?**
10. **In which year was the *Catholic Emancipation Act* passed?**

Discussion:
Debate the following within groups.
Find quotes, references or passages from books that back up your argument.

1. Women have smaller brains than men.
2. Educating women reduces jobs available for men.

A BRIEF HISTORY OF EDUCATION

Education features prominently throughout the story of *Jane Eyre*. There are two main reasons for this: Charlotte Brontë had herself attended school (school was not compulsory during her lifetime) which lead to a short career as a teacher. Secondly, it was one of the few respectable careers that women could have and this fitted in with her principles of female independence. The benefits of education are well known today, but this wasn't always the case; and as with many things we now take for granted, the largest changes took place during the reign of Queen Victoria (1837 – 1901).

Pre-Victorian Schooling

Before the 19th Century, education was only for the rich and privileged minority. However, toward 1800, a concerted effort was made by the Church to establish "Charity Schools", enabling the poor to receive a basic education. The "National Society" (for Promoting the Education of the Poor in the Principles of the Established Church throughout England and Wales) was established in 1811 with the aim of providing a school in every parish that would "teach the children of the nation to be literate, numerate and skilled to enter employment, and to provide a specifically Christian education".

In the story, Lowood School was a Church School. Charlotte based it on her experiences at the Clergy Daughters' School, Cowan Bridge, founded in 1824 by Rev. W Wilson (on whom Brontë based the character of Mr Brocklehurst). In her short time there, she saw two of her sisters Elizabeth and Maria fall ill and quickly die at home (Maria was the inspiration for Helen Burns in the book). As Charlotte did in real life, Jane Eyre goes on to become a teacher; in the novel, that is at the Church School in Morton.

As Church Schools became more commonplace, rich families began to employ a governess to educate their children (just as Rochester employed Jane Eyre as a governess to teach Adèle). Upper class boys often then progressed to public school, which concentrated as much on sporting activities as they did on academic subjects. Middle class boys tended to go to grammar school, while girls wanting more than a basic education went to private girls' schools.

The Victorian Age

Society was already changing radically when Queen Victoria came to the throne in 1837. She effectively continued to oversee the industrial revolution, as the world moved away from agriculture toward manufacturing. That change encouraged a movement of people away from the countryside and into the growing cities – but the growth in the number of children within each parish of these densely populated areas meant that Church Schools were inadequate. More schools were created in the form of Charity Schools which were not directly connected with the Church. These so-called "Ragged Schools" survived on donations made by wealthy patrons and local businesses.

Raising money for Ragged Schools was difficult and a lack of funds restricted the schools' ability to provide a decent education for its pupils. This was resolved in 1870, when schools were given the ability to obtain funding from local town rates. This marked the beginning of the modern education system. By 1881, schooling became compulsory from ages 5 to 10, even if it had to be paid for; but in 1891 this level of education became free for everyone. By the end of the century, the school leaving age had been raised to 12 (it was finally raised to 16 in 1972).

KNOW YOUR ABCs

Write A, B or C in the Answer column

No.	Question	Answer
1	Jane Eyre went to work as a governess and taught Rochester's ward Adèle. This would indicate that Rochester was: a) poor b) rich c) in need of a babysitter	
2	In 1901 the school leaving age was: a) 9 b) 10 c) 12	
3	During the industrial revolution, there was a shift in the population from rural areas toward: a) towns and cities b) the seaside c) the mountains	
4	Charlotte Brontë attended which school: a) She didn't attend school b) Parsonage Ragged School c) The Clergy Daughters' School	
5	*Jane Eyre* was first published in 1847. Who was the reigning monarch at that time? a) Queen Victoria b) Queen Elizabeth I c) King William IV	

JANE EYRE CHAPTER BY CHAPTER SYNOPSIS

Section 1 Gateshead (November – January)

1. Jane Eyre is a passionate and imaginative ten-year-old orphan living with her Aunt Reed and cousins John, Eliza and Georgina. They exclude and bully her, and she has no option but to take it. She is reading a book full of doleful landscapes and scary birds on her own when John throws a book at her, causing her to hit her head. Bleeding, she gets the better of the fourteen-year-old boy in a fight but is reported by the sisters to "Mama." Aunt Reed, as always, blames Jane, and she is hauled away to the red room by the servants Bessie and Abbot.

2. "Mad cat" Jane is made to sit still in a chair behind the locked doors of this unused room. She fumes but grows gradually frightened as dusk falls. Her uncle John died here, and, because his deathbed instruction to Aunt Reed to care for Jane has been ignored, she fears his ghost will haunt it. She screams for help. Bessie and Abbot answer, but Aunt Reed insists she stays imprisoned for another hour. She faints.

3. Mr. Lloyd, the servants' apothecary (not the family doctor) is called to treat Jane. She wakes to his care and to Bessie's peace offering of tarts and books. She refuses these but tries to explain her miserable state to Mr. Lloyd. He suggests going to her father's family, but she assumes they are beggars and chooses his other suggestion – to go away to boarding school.

4. Aunt Reed approves the boarding school plan: anything to get Jane off her hands. A "black pillar" visits – the owner/headmaster of the school Jane is going to – and she is mortified by the report given of her character. In an outburst that strikes terror into her guardian, she says she will never call her "Aunt" again. Bessie privately approves this new spirit, and Jane makes up with the story-telling nursemaid of her childhood.

Section 2 Lowood school (8 years)

5. Jane travels all day through bitter winter weather to Lowood and goes to bed unfed. Next day, the breakfast porridge is burnt and no one can eat it. Against orders, the headmistress, Miss Temple, requests a lunch of bread and cheese to be served. Jane meets Helen Burns, who tells her all about the school.

6. Jane joins class four and begins with a sewing lesson. She watches Helen Burns being picked on in a history lesson and accepting both unfair criticism (Helen is good at history) and unfair punishment (she is flogged!) without complaint. This bewilders the righteously indignant Jane, but Helen dreamily explains that Christians should welcome suffering. Jane will learn from, if only ever partly accept, this attitude.

7. In common with all the girls at Lowood, Jane suffers from cold and hunger and resents the older girls who monopolize both food and fire. Mr. Brocklehurst visits and attacks Miss Temple for the two lunches given out on burnt porridge days, Julia Severn for having naturally curly hair (his own daughters artificially curl theirs!) and Jane – in front of the whole school – for being the liar Aunt Reed claims she is.

JANE EYRE CHAPTER BY CHAPTER SYNOPSIS

8. Helen Burns and Miss Temple help Jane to control a rage which (as in chapter one) might have made things worse. After breaking down in tears, Jane tells Miss Temple her side of the story. The teacher checks this version with Mr. Lloyd, who confirms it, thereby clearing her name to the whole school, and moves her to a higher class. Jane is stronger and more self-possessed whenever ill treated in her life from then on.

9. A typhus epidemic breaks out in Lowood caused by the weather, poor living conditions and marshy location. ("Semi starvation and neglected colds had predisposed most of the pupils to receive infection: forty-five out of the eighty girls lay ill at one time.") Helen – never strong – contracts the disease. Jane insists on seeing her in the sick bay and spends the last night of Helen's life with her. Helen does not fear death, but welcomes it. Jane is more keen on life. Jane sleeps. Helen dies.

10. Chapters one to nine cover less than six months. Chapter ten covers eight years. Lowood is reformed because of the epidemic, and Mr. Brocklehurst loses overall charge. Jane rises (after six years) to become assistant teacher. But when Miss Temple leaves to marry a clergyman, the eighteen-year-old Jane suddenly wants to escape from Lowood and see life beyond its narrow hills. She secures a job as a governess to a little girl at Thornfield Hall, earning double her Lowood salary (£30 a year). The day before leaving, Bessie arrives with the information – which Jane was never given – that seven years ago Jane's uncle was looking for her at Gateshead before going abroad.

Section 3: Thornfield, October? – July? (a month after midsummer)

11. Jane travels all day and evening to her new employment at Thornfield Hall. She meets and likes her new "employer" Mrs. Fairfax but learns next day that her real employer is the popular Mr. Rochester, who is often absent. Her pupil, a little French girl named Adèle Varens, is his ward. Jane hears a blood-curdling laugh from the attic as she is being given a tour of the house. No one mentions it, but there is something spooky about the house despite the warm welcome, and the reference to Bluebeard (a man who murdered his wives) reinforces this.

12. Settled in her new job and home – drawn in bored moments up near the attic or outside for walks – Jane longs for excitement. She finds it in a lonely lane on her way to mail a letter, when a mysterious rider and a dog she half-believes is the legendary "Gytrash" burst upon her out of the icy dusk. The rider slips, badly injures his ankle and is forced to request her help. She helps him, not realizing it is her employer, Mr. Rochester. She continues on her way to Hay.

JANE EYRE CHAPTER BY CHAPTER SYNOPSIS

13. Thornfield is brought alive by Rochester's presence and his visitors. At last, in the evening, Jane and Adèle are invited to meet Jane's mysterious and rather surly employer. Jane has to demonstrate her skills on the piano (poor) and in painting (inspired) – wild emotional paintings very like those in the book she read in chapter one.

14. Rochester deliberately ignores Jane for several days and then invites her (and Adèle) to spend an evening with him. He gives Adèle her "cadeaux" (toys and a dress). Jane and Rochester exchange witty banter about his ugliness, behavior and social superiority.

15. Jane and Rochester walk together in the grounds of the hall and exchange stories. Rochester explains Adèle and why she is his ward. Jane lies awake thinking about him, grateful for his company and cheer. She hears a strange noise from the attic and, going to Rochester's room, finds him asleep with his bed in flames. She saves him. Rochester reveals the arsonist as Grace Poole, the servant Jane has seen in the attic. Rochester expresses great affection toward Jane – "strange fire was in his look" – not just gratitude.

16. Jane is puzzled to find Grace Poole repairing the damage in Rochester's room. She warns Jane to keep her bedroom locked at night. Jane seeks out Rochester for an explanation, but he has gone to visit some "fine friends" and (worse for Jane) ladies. Jane's growing confidence in her attractiveness to Rochester is shattered: she could never be his wife. She paints a self-portrait of her "poor, plain, unconnected" self to put herself back in her real place.

17. A fortnight passes, and Rochester and his fine friends and ladies come to Thornfield. The secret of the attic arsonist is kept from Jane (and thus also from us). The guests bring excitement, hustle and bustle, and on the second day Jane and Adèle are invited to join the fine folk after dinner. The ladies snipe at "governesses." Jane leaves, but Rochester pursues and orders her to attend after dinner every night.

18. The fine guests play charades and hint continually of marriage between Rochester and the beautiful, "strapping and buxom" Miss Ingram – (though such a marriage would itself be a charade). In Rochester's absence, a stranger called Mr. Mason arrives. A gypsy calls to tell the ladies' fortunes, including Jane's. Miss Ingram does not enjoy her fortune, or Jane's inclusion in the game.

19. The gypsy interrogates Jane about the house party rather than telling her fortune, but she does "read" her face. Jane realises the old gypsy is really Mr. Rochester. Rochester is dismayed when told of Mr. Mason's arrival. Is the secret of Thornfield about to be revealed?

20. A harrowing scream comes from the room above Jane. The guests awake, and Rochester reassures them. He secretly takes Jane up to the attic to nurse Mr. Mason, who has been stabbed. She waits with him until dawn for Rochester to return, as mystified as the reader. Mr. Mason is taken away. Rochester talks about the falseness of society's morals; Jane says she will obey Rochester in anything that is "right." He announces his attention to marry Miss Ingram.

JANE EYRE CHAPTER BY CHAPTER SYNOPSIS

21. Jane has nightly dreams about a baby – a bad omen. A dying Aunt Reed summons her to Gateshead, and Rochester reluctantly allows her to go. (Jane asks him to help find her another job before he marries.) Bessie welcomes her; Eliza and Georgina don't; John has mysteriously died of indulgence. The confused Aunt Reed eventually gives her a letter from her uncle John offering to adopt her – it is three years old. Jane forgives Aunt Reed (as the "perfect Helen Burns" might have taught Jane by example), but the forgiveness is not accepted or returned, and Jane accepts that they can never really be reconciled. Aunt Reed dies, rejecting Jane's hand but clinging to her view of Jane as an impossible child.

22. Jane leaves Gateshead after a month. Georgina will marry for fortune and Eliza retreat from the world into a moral fortress as a Catholic nun. (The two kinds of Victorian femininity – but Jane is neither). Jane realizes that Rochester (and Thornfield) is her only real home and, returning to it one evening in all of its summer glory (rather than its spooky horror), tells him so. The marriage to Miss Ingram remains in the background but seems more rumor than fact.

23. Jane walks the Eden-like grounds of Thornfield on Midsummer Eve. She bumps into Rochester. He says she must leave as soon as he is married, and she cries under the old chestnut tree. But he means she must leave for her honeymoon with him: He is proposing. Jane is overwhelmed but finally accepts. They kiss. That night, a thunderbolt splits the old chestnut in two. Not a good omen.

24. Rochester overwhelms Jane with flattery, gifts, shopping trips for jewels and dresses, and plans for a honeymoon tour of Europe. Or he tries to – she is uncomfortable and aware that Mrs. Fairfax shares her fears. Jane writes to her uncle for money and keeps her job as governess – both acts assert her independence. Jane also keeps Rochester at a decent distance the whole month of their engagement. As the chestnut tree incident suggested, something is very wrong.

25. Jane waits by the old chestnut tree for Rochester to return from business. She has awful news. Amid desolate dreams the previous night (of Thornfield reduced to a burnt out shell) she was awoken by a ghost in her room, and the ghost actually tore the wedding veil Rochester gave her in two. Rochester laughs it off – it's only Grace Poole. The night before her wedding, Jane sleeps in the nursery with Adèle.

26. The wedding begins in haste and without guests. It is interrupted by a solicitor who announces that Rochester is already married to Bertha. Her brother, Mason, confirms this. Rochester takes the church party up to the attic to see the locked up beast his mad wife has become, one whom its jailer Grace Poole's occasional drunkenness allows to wander free. It is Jane's letter to uncle John (who worked for Mason) that alerted Mason to Rochester's plans to remarry. Jane hides away in her room.

27. Jane agonizes all night but knows she must leave her "master." Rochester pleads against this, giving the full story of his "honey-trap" marriage and offering her a pampered position as his mistress. Following her Lowood-trained conscience, she resists this offer, despite all of the passionate longing and love she has for him. In the red room, the lonely and unloved child Jane lacked all self-control. Here, she has learned it. She escapes in the night and pays a coachman all the money she has to get as far away as possible.

JANE EYRE CHAPTER BY CHAPTER SYNOPSIS

Section Four: Moor End, Moor House, July – January?

28. Jane is at a crossroads – Whitcross – in the middle of desolate moors. She sleeps there, like an animal. Next day she seeks work all day and finally resorts to begging. She sleeps in a wood, fails again to find work all day, and returns to the moors desperate and starving. She stumbles on an isolated farmhouse – a picture of domestic bliss – but a servant woman, Hannah, refuses her entry or help. The young master, St. John, by contrast, takes her in.

29. Jane is in a high fever for three days. She recovers and helps the servant with housework, learning about the family. They are St. John, Mary and Diana Rivers, come to sort out the affairs of a recently deceased relative, old Mr. John Rivers. Mary and Diana have been working as governesses; St. John is vicar of Morton, the hamlet Jane begged in. She asks to keep her own story secret – revealing only that she was a governess and asking to be called Jane Elliot. The Rivers family are mirror images/opposites of the Reed children.

30. Jane, Mary and Diana become warm friends, almost sisters. St. John is more distant and intimidating. He offers Jane work as a schoolmistress in a school he is setting up at Morton. Despite some snobbery about teaching cottage girls, Jane accepts this chance to be independent. The Rivers' uncle has just died and left them out of his will because of a quarrel with their father, and their occupation of Moor House is only temporary.

31. Jane moves to her new schoolroom and its cottage in Morton. On that first solitary evening, she desperately misses Rochester, though she knows she was right to leave him. St. John visits her and explains his plan to become a missionary. The school's beautiful benefactress, Miss Rosamond Oliver, interrupts, and her attraction to and for St. John is clear: they are made for each other, but St. John keeps his feelings rigidly hidden.

32. Jane is a success at the local school by day but dreams with acute longing of Rochester at night. St. John also teaches at the school and is often visited there by Miss Oliver. Miss Oliver befriends Jane, visits her cottage and has her beautiful portrait done there. St. John admires the portrait, and Jane quizzes him about his feelings for its subject. St. John tears a piece of paper from the portrait as he leaves.

33. It is Christmas. A fairy tale comes true as St. John brings the news that Jane has been left £20,000 (the strip of paper – a signature – was confirmation of her real name) by the very uncle who has disinherited the Rivers family. She and St. John share an uncle, Old John Rivers. Jane now has a fortune but more importantly, the family she always lacked. She shares the £20,000 between the four of them.

JANE EYRE CHAPTER BY CHAPTER SYNOPSIS

34. The Rivers family, including Jane, go back to Moor House for Christmas – Jane and Hannah's efforts to make it Christmassy are appreciated by the sisters but ignored by St. John, who insists Jane travel to school through impossible winter weather and learn Hindustani instead of the German she and Diana enjoy. He kisses her cheek. Jane writes two unanswered letters to Mrs. Fairfax asking after Rochester and fears the worst. In the following summer, St. John proposes marriage and a life as a missionary with him in India. Almost overpowered by his certainty, Jane agrees to the latter but not the former saying he doesn't love her. They part in cold politeness, which upsets her.

35. St. John continues to freeze Jane out, and they argue. Jane explains the situation to Diana, who supports her, predicting (correctly) that India would kill her. After prayers, St. John proposes again, and Jane feels in the same situation as with Rochester, "as hard beset by him now as I had been once before, in a different way, by another." She very nearly gives in, but asks God for help. She suddenly hears Rochester's voice "calling" her name.

Section 5: Ferndean (month of arrival January? – present time of writing)

36. Jane travels next day by coach to Thornfield but finds only the burnt shell her dreams once showed her. She hears from a local that there has been a fire, caused by Bertha, and that Rochester has been maimed and blinded trying – and failing – to save her. Very sure of herself now, at last, Jane orders a carriage to take her to Rochester's new and smaller home at Ferndean.

37. Jane arrives at Ferndean at dusk and glimpses Rochester outside. She arranges with the two servants to take him his candles and glass of water, pretending to be the maid. The ruse works, and in an atmosphere of teasing but also of deep emotion, the two lovers are reunited. They sup together, and next morning she fills him in on the complete Rivers story, including St. John's offer. He proposes – but not in the frivolous/bigamist way he did before – and this time she accepts him.

38. "Reader, I married him." After a quiet wedding, Rochester and Jane live "happily ever after" at Ferndean, mutually devoted and mutually dependent equals. He depends on her eyes but does partially recover his sight in time to see their son. She shares all this news by letter with Diana and Mary – who later also marry – and with St. John who is now in India and remains single. They occasionally correspond. The novel ends not with Jane and Rochester's perfect marriage but with St. John waiting for death in India.

UNDERSTANDING THE NOVEL

TEST YOUR UNDERSTANDING
1. Who proposes to Jane?
2. What happened to Jane's parents?
3. Which school did Jane attend?
4. Name five locations in which the story takes place.
5. Name all of the Rivers family.
6. What was the name of Rochester's dog? 
7. Where did Bertha come from?
8. Who was Mrs. Fairfax? And Adèle?
9. Who was Rochester rumored to be about to marry?
10. What happens to St. John?

JANE EYRE QUIZ

Circle your choice

1. Jane lives – until she is 10 – in (a) Harrogate? (b) Watergate? (c) Gateshead? (d) Newgate?

2. Her first home is (a) an orphanage? (b) a school for clergymen's daughters? (c) a foster care home? (d) the mansion of her uncle's family?

3. What is an apothecary?
(a) Medical practitioner. (b) A social worker. (c) A clergyman. (d) A truant officer.

4. Aunt Reed promised her husband (a) to give Jane an education? (b) to raise her as one of her own? (c) to find her a husband? (d) to put her in touch with her uncle?

5. Lowood is (a) a charity school for female orphans? (b) a prison? (c) a borstal? (d) a lunatic asylum?

6. Who is Jane's first close friend? (a) Eliza Reed. (b) Bessie. (c) Miss Temple.(d) Helen Burns.

7. Which of the following characters says he might bend Jane "like a reed"?
(a) John Reed. (b) Rochester. (c) Brocklehurst. (d) St. John Rivers.

8. Which of the following elements is NOT represented in characters' names and/or natures?
(a) Air. (b) Earth. (b) Fire. (d) Water.

9. Who describes Jane as a "servant and agent" of Satan?
(a) St. John Rivers. (b) Aunt Reed. (c) Blanche Ingram. (d) Brocklehurst.

10. Which of these descriptions best fits Jane? (a) a "witch". (b) a "little wife". (c) "a queer, frightened, shy little thing". (d) "an independent woman…[her] own mistress."

11. Who says this to Rochester: "I have not been buried with inferior minds, and excluded from every glimpse of communion with what is bright and energetic and high…I have talked face to face with what I reverence…with an original, a vigorous, an expanded mind"?
(a) Jane. (b) Blanche. (c) Bertha. (d) Mrs. Fairfax.

12. "The last letter I received from him drew from my eyes human tears, and yet filled my heart with Divine joy". What does Jane mean? (a) that she is sad that Rochester is blind and lame but at least God has given them a happy marriage. (b) that St. John's marriage proposal upsets her but she still likes the idea of being his female curate. (c) that she's sad St. John is dying but glad for him because he will get his "sure reward" in heaven. (d) that she thanks God for her Uncle John willing her £20,000 even though she's sad he's dead.

WHAT HAPPENS NEXT?

TASK:

Look closely at the pictures on each card in the following pages. In the box, write down what you think is happening in each scene. You need to have read the novel first!

Comic Card	**WHAT IS HAPPENING?** Describe in your own words. Try to explain what is going on in each panel and what the characters are saying. Can you remember what happens next?
Card 1	
Card 2	
Card 3	
Card 4	

COMIC CARD 1

Chapter VII

COMIC CARD 2

Chapter XXIII

COMIC CARD 3

Chapter XXXV

COMIC CARD 4

Chapter XXXVII

WHAT HAPPENS NEXT?

TASK 2:

Look again at Comic Card 4. Cut out the blank word balloons below and write in them the words that you think the characters are saying to each other.

You should:

– Make sure that the "tail" of the balloon is pointing at the correct character.
– Make sure that the word balloons follow from left to right so that you can follow the conversation easily.
– When you are sure that you have them in the right place, stick the word balloons to the sheet.

You could:

– Write the exact words from the novel (this might be difficult to fit in!)
– Write the words in modern English.
– Make up your own words for the characters, but make sure that they are still saying the same sort of thing to each other.
– Write in what the characters are THINKING rather than saying.

There are more word balloons than you need here. You could draw your own if you prefer.

JANE EYRE

WORKSHEET 1

Victorian readers on the whole expected their heroines to be pretty and rich – and if possible glamorous and grand as well – the way we like our pop and film stars. If the heroine wasn't rich and preferably posh as well, she must at least be pretty. Jane was quite a surprise for them, and not just because a woman and not a man is at the center telling her own story, but because she is also "plain, poor and little." Some early readers complained that they could find nothing to love in her, nor any reason Mr. Rochester should be so deeply in love with her. This is not just to do with her lack of beauty – her flinty character was also criticized – but her lack of beauty strongly affected how that character is seen. Even today, when films are made of *Jane Eyre*, the director often finds it difficult to make Jane appealing without also making her pretty.

There had already been novels, like *Pamela*, in which suffering heroines told their own stories. But *Pamela* was written by a man, and his heroine was not only exceptionally pretty but also perfectly behaved. Jane Austen definitely put women's stories on the literary map, but only her last novel, *Persuasion,* attempted to make a (stubborn) woman no longer young and beautiful its heroine. Charlotte Brontë was determined to invent a heroine with other qualities than looks and cash and glamour. She wanted her character to be a woman one could meet in real life. Once the surprise died down, more and more early readers were impressed. One called Jane "A creature of flesh and blood, with very fleshly infirmities, and very mortal excellencies, a woman, not a pattern." Another praised Jane's "kindness of heart and perseverance" and her "triumph over every obstacle."

TASK: **Is Jane a successful heroine?**

Discuss your thoughts in a group.

When reading, what qualities do you look for in a heroine (or hero) ?

Give examples of at least five heroines (and heroes) in books you've read

Name of heroine (or hero)	**What did you honestly like about her (him)?** **How important is the heroine's looks?**

Is Jane an interesting heroine? Say why.	**What qualities do you like about her?**

JANE EYRE

WORKSHEET 2

In modern books – less so, still, in films – we are used to real life heroines (and heroes) who are not saints or even conventional beauties. We accept "character" narrators who might not be perfect, and we like them for it. We like reality in the way they live – in ordinary streets – and the way they are – stroppy, misunderstood, even behaviorally challenged! The fits of rage Jane has against John and Mrs. Reed and Mr. Brocklehurst could come out of such a book. "The little Jane with her sharp eyes and dogmatic speeches, is a being you neither could fondle nor love" is how one early reader put it, sounding rather like Brocklehurst or Aunt Reed herself. Jane's world is harsh and abusive in a way that was all too real and common for a child of her Victorian background.

But part of Jane's attraction is that while "a creature of flesh and blood," she is also more than ordinary. Rochester calls her an "elf," and magical things seem to happen to and around her. (The love of the forty-year-old Rochester for a girl under twenty is compared to being "bewitched".) She is a real orphan but sometimes seems like an orphan in a fairy story, like Cinderella, in fact, though without the blonde curls and blue eyes.

TASK:

Jane Eyre: a fairy tale heroine?

Look at the following episodes of the story in groups and decide how much is real and how much is fairy tale.

Episode: location, description of episode and comments.	**Fairy tale or realism or both?** Rate the episode 1–5 where 5 is total realism and 1 is total fairy tale. Explain your rating.
Gateshead: (a) Jane is an orphan and a dependant in the house of a selfish, hard-hearted aunt, thrown upon the cruelty of relations who neglect and abuse her. Victorian society with its very high birth rates and very high death rates produced many more orphans than we have now. Orphans were one of the main issues of the age and a common subject of Victorian novels.	(a)
(b) Locked in the "red room," with its "certain secret drawer in the wardrobe" (in which documents to do with Jane are hidden?) on a moonlit night, Jane sees her own spooky reflection in a looking-glass, "with a white face and arms specking the gloom and glittering eyes of fear moving where all else was still (like) a real spirit…one of the tiny phantoms, half fairy, half imp." And then – as her raging blood cools, believing "Mr. Reed's spirit" has returned to avenge her – "a gleam from a lantern" which "prepared as my mind was for horror…I thought…was a…vision from another world…I thought a ghost would come". She screams in terror, a scream that in turn terrifies her guards. But her (later, adult) narrator does not say it was a ghost, only that her child's mind believed it was.	(b)

JANE EYRE

(c) Wakes up in front of a "terrible red glare, crossed with thick black bars" surrounded by "a hollow sound…as if muffled by a rush of wind or water… terror confused my faculties...(but) I was in my own bed, and...the red glare was the nursery fire." The description is like Victorian descriptions of hell: the child may believe she's gone there, but the adult narrator corrects this.	(c)
(d) "Shaking from head to foot, thrilled with ungovernable excitement," Jane retaliates after her aunt slanders her to Mr. Brocklehurst… "Mrs. Reed looked frightened…she was lifting up her hands, rocking herself to and fro, and even twisting her face as if she would cry. ...A ridge of lit heath, alive, glancing, devouring, would have been a meet emblem of my mind when I accused and menaced Mrs. Reed." Though Bessie prefers this new Jane and finds her less provoking than the "start" of the previously "queer, frightened, shy little thing" at being spoken to sharply, this rage expresses the Jane she has become: revengeful and superstitious and almost supernaturally threatening. A "discord at Gateshead Hall." **Lowood:** this whole section has often been praised for its extreme realism. Many Victorian documents, as well as documentary novels, describe schools exactly like this. Can you find any "fairy tale" elements? Is there still a touch of Cinderella here?	(d)
Thornfield: find the following folk/fairy tale elements in Jane's experiences: a magical dog, a Prince, a fortune teller, a fairy tale proposal (one early reader called this "Conduct hardly proper between a single man and a maid in her teens"), a haunting, a vampire, a Bluebeard's wife, a visit to hell, a fairy godmother? In each case, is there also a realistic explanation? What is it? One has been completed for you.	(a) There **is** what Jane calls a "foul German spectre, the vampyr" – it bites Mason in the attic and Jane actually has to nurse Mason afterwards until the light of dawn. There are other descriptions of the same creature in terms of devil and beast. But before the days of "sectioning," dangerously insane family members of the upper classes were often secreted in remote mansions. One early reviewer wrote, "Neither is the mystery of Thornfield an exaggeration of reality. We, ourselves, know of a large mansion-house in a distant county where, for many years, a miscreant was kept in close confinement… only darkly hinted at in the neighbourhood." (H.F. Chorley, 1847).

JANE EYRE

Moor House/ Morton: Jane, by complete chance, and at death's door, stumbles in the middle of a remote moor upon long lost (and now – like her – orphaned) cousins who are the mirror reverse image of the Reeds. Then a fortune is left to Jane (Jane Heir) – at Christmas – by a long lost uncle. Out of the blue, she gets the ready–made family she's always lacked and independence. Fairy tale happy endings?

Ferndean: And they all lived happily ever after? Can you find any examples where Jane is clearly a real woman living in a real Victorian world rather than a fairy tale princess in fairy tale heaven? (Hint: would her husband have gotten a new hand and all his sight back in a traditional fairy tale?)

JANE THE TEACHER

WORKSHEET 3

Jane is learning throughout the story. She goes away to Lowood for an education and certainly gets one, going quickly to the top of her first class and after six years becoming a teacher there herself. But what she really learns at Lowood (from Helen Burns and Miss Temple) is a lesson for life. She learns that patience and principle, rather than "passion" (or rage), is the best response to wretched conditions.

TASK:

Think

Most of us learn lessons for life in school that aren't taught in the school curriculum. Think for a moment about what you have learned at school so far that isn't "set" as a subject.

We don't see Jane's actual teaching at Lowood, but she doubtless passes on the patience she has learned. In pairs, discuss what kind of teacher she is. Strict? Kind? Both? What would it be like to be in her lessons? Role-play her helping a pupil with a difficult lesson.

After two years, when Miss Temple leaves, patience is no longer enough for Jane. She is bored and wants adventure. She gets a job as a governess to Adèle at Thornfield, at double the salary. It is here with Adèle and at the Morton school later in the book that we are shown what Jane's teaching is like.

Examples of Jane's teaching	**What kind of teacher/person is Jane?**
Jane's 8-year-old pupil at Thornfield is an opera dancer's illegitimate daughter, frivolous, pretty, pampered and French. Brontë's creation of this child was much praised at the time. She is the very opposite of Jane and Lowood pupils Jane taught. Though she is unparented (like Jane and many at Lowood) she is otherwise more like the Reed children. "She had finished her breakfast, so I permitted her to give a specimen of her accomplishments." Now, shall I dance for you?" "No, that will do." "I found my pupil sufficiently docile, though disinclined to apply: she had not been used to regular occupation of any kind. I felt it would be injudicious to confine her too much at first; so, when I had talked to her a good deal, and got her to learn a little, and when the morning had advanced to noon, I allowed her to return to her nurse."	Is Jane strict (as Lowood was) or lax (as Adèle is evidently used to)? Answer these questions to help you decide: 1. Underline any words that suggest Jane is very much in control of her pupil. 2. In a different color, underline any words that suggest Adèle is disobedient or out of Jane's control. 3. Underline in a third color any words and phrases that describe what actually happened or was learned in the morning's lesson. When you have decided on how strict or lax Jane is, explain whether you think she is a good teacher or not. Imagine "Gateshead" Jane, at 18, trying to teach Adèle: what has Jane added to her people skills in those Lowood years?

JANE THE TEACHER

Jane's feelings about teaching the cottage girls of Morton are described three times at three stages: the openings of chapters 31, 32 and 34. Read these pages now and locate the following thoughts and phrases.

1. (Jane's first day at Morton) "Some of them are unmannered, rough, intractable, as well as ignorant; but others are docile, have a wish to learn… I felt degraded…weakly dismayed at the ignorance, the poverty, the coarseness of all I heard and saw around me."	1. Tell the story of Jane's first day from the point of view of one of the "unmannered, rough and ignorant" girls. Make up an example of something she said to you and something she tried to teach you. Did she succeed? Decide what you think of your new teacher – they say she is an ex-governess who lives with a gentleman and ladies and that her last pupil was a little rich kid from Paris. What's she doing with the likes of you? Is she a snob? Is she just "slumming" to please the missionary Mr. Rivers? Is she a "do gooder" like him? Or does she just need the money? Someone says she was seen begging in Morton a few weeks ago.
2. (after a short while there) "I found some of these heavy-looking, gaping rustics wake up into sharp-witted girls…these soon took a pleasure in doing their work well…in acquiring quiet and orderly manners…the rapidity of their progress…was even surprising…I began personally to like some of the best girls and they liked me…I became a favorite in the neighborhood. Wherever I went out, I heard on all sides cordial salutations."	2. Continue the story in the words of the same girl but now "woken up into a sharp-witted girl." You now really like your new teacher and even wave to her in the street. And you're really good at schoolwork. How did she manage this? Was she strict or easy going?
3. (at the end of the first term) "I stood with the key in my hand, exchanging a few words of special farewell with some half-dozen of my best scholars: as decent, respectable, modest, and well-informed young women as could be found in the ranks of the British peasantry…since those days I have seen paysannes and Baueriinen; and the best of them seemed to me ignorant, coarse and besotted compared with my Morton girls. "And you have only toiled a few months! (said St. John) Would not a life devoted to the task of regenerating your race be well spent?" "Yes…but it could not go on for ever so: I want to enjoy my own faculties as well as to cultivate those of other people."	3. Miss Eyre is leaving, hopefully just for the Christmas holidays. She stayed behind after school to say goodbye to you and five other of her best scholars. There's a rumor she's leaving forever – you heard her tell Mr. Rivers she wanted to "enjoy her own faculties as well," and of course she's come into money lately. You heard Mr. Rivers coaxing her to stay, and you hope she will. He asks you to use your new learning to write her a letter asking her to stay. You agree. Write this letter, telling her all the ways she's improved you as a scholar and a person and arguing why she should stay. 4. Underline all the adjectives Jane uses to describe pupils in the column opposite and arrange them into positive and negative columns.

THE REEDS

Jane's first – false – family are the Reeds. They are a "gentry" family, quite rich, their work done by servants; they are the owners of Gateshead Hall. Their name – "Reed" – is suggestive. Later in the novel, when he is trying (and failing) to bend Jane to his will, Rochester will say, "A mere reed she feels in my hand" Jane is also "pliant as a reed" under (St. John's) potent "kindness." The associations are with weakness, and both these qualities particularly appear in Aunt Reed and John.

TASK 1:

Group Discussion

Read chapters 1 – 4. What kind of parent is Aunt Reed?

Now look up the pages that describe how her children turn out.

How did Mrs. Reed's parenting influence the personalities of her children?

TASK 2:

Jane's first "family" – Comprehension and Debate

For the following, you will need quotes from the description of John, from John's attack on Jane and from the description of weak Reed family parenting (her children… "defied her authority and laughed it to scorn") versus Jane's apparent strength. You will also be looking up the details of John's decline and death, of Jane's last meeting (after eight years) with her false first family, and of the death of Aunt Reed.

1. Read the description of John in chapter 1. How old is John? Give three details of his personal appearance.
2. Aunt Reed believes her son's "delicate health" has suffered from working too hard at school and ("perhaps") from missing home. What are the real reasons for his poor health?
3. What words or phrases can you find that suggest that both Aunt Reed and John share poor vision.
4. What evidence is there that Jane, on the contrary, is eagle-eyed?
5. Find three examples of weak parenting.
6. Quote one example of Jane's strength of character.
7. Can you find any general similarities between John Reed's life and Rochester's? Differences?
8. Georgiana and Eliza first lose their brother and then their mother. What evidence can you find that the family does not exactly come together and support each other in their loss?
9. What do they eventually do with their lives?

TASK 3:

Debate the following in groups.

"All three Reed children are weak victims of a weak upbringing." Find a quote (or two) to back up your answer.

BROCKLEHURST AND ST. JOHN RIVERS

Jane has a lot of trouble with these two clergymen, who represent two aspects of religion: the worldly and the ascetic. Charlotte Brontë was herself a clergyman's daughter and received proposals from three different clergymen in her time. She knew something about them.

Brocklehurst is a hypocrite. He believes devoutly in Christian self-denial, but only for other people (i.e. the girls in his charity school). He himself is a snob, swayed by money and status.

St. John Rivers is a Calvinist missionary, a strange mixture of self-denial and selfishness, but not a hypocrite. His restless ambition combines heavenly zeal and earthly pride.

TASK:

Discussion

Debate the following within groups. Find quotes that back up your argument.

Brocklehurst

1. Brocklehurst looks like "a black pillar" to Jane. What qualities does he have in common with stone?
2. Would Brocklehurst instruct his own daughter's topknots to be cut off?
3. Would Brocklehurst order his own daughters to "be children of grace"?
4. Does Brocklehurst understand children?
5. In the Bible, Jesus says, "suffer little children to come unto me," and Bessie's song speaks of "only angels" caring for orphans. Is there anything of these in Lowood?
6. Consider the notion: Brocklehurst believes in self-denial – but only for other people.

St. John

1. Find one similarity and one difference between St. John and Brocklehurst.
2. Does St. John ever show Christian love to anyone?
3. List five people St. John might be expected to love. Does he?
4. What qualities, if any, are admirable in St. John?
5. What qualities are repulsive?
6. What is suggested by Rochester answering Jane's prayer - with St. John standing by claiming to be the voice of God?
7. Consider the notion: St. John's religion is just another word for suicide.

HELEN BURNS AND MISS TEMPLE

TASK 1:

Pairs. Look again at the Lowood section of the novel. Brocklehurst's "worldly" religion is put to shame by the genuinely spiritual – and truly loving - Helen Burns, a victim of a so-called "charitable" school. She is not in the novel long but leaves a profound and troubling impression. Discuss the impact she has on Jane's life and on us, the reader.

Miss Temple's cool demeanor is a useful training for the fiery and passionate child Jane. She is called Temple, and Jane certainly worships her. But once she leaves Lowood, Jane never thinks of or mentions her again. It is a subtle portrait, but it may be argued that Miss Temple, like a temple, has something of the stoniness of the two clergymen in the novel – Brocklehurst (a black pillar) and St. John (white marble). What do you think?

TASK 2:

Imagine you are Jane during your first winter at Lowood. Write her diary entries, making sure you include the following:

(a) your very first impressions – of the cold, the porridge, the hunger, of the older girls menacing you for your food and coffee.
(b) your early impressions of Helen Burns and Miss Temple.
(c) the incident when Brocklehurst humiliates you and how Helen and Miss Temple advise you.
(d) the typhus epidemic and your last night with Helen – including what it was like to wake up and find her dead.

TASK 3:

Eight years pass. Write the farewell dialog between Miss Temple and her favorite pupil, who is now a junior colleague, on Miss Temple's wedding day. Remember Miss Temple would be kind and warm and ready with good advice, as always setting a good example, but wouldn't get carried away. Perhaps Jane would like her to, remembering the teacher she once worshipped?
Or is Jane – who has also outgrown Lowood - secretly more interested in the man Miss Temple is marrying?

ROCHESTER

"The reader cannot see anything loveable in Mr. R, nor why he should be so deeply in love with Jane Eyre."

"Strange energy was in his voice; strange fire in his look."

"I both wished and feared to see Mr. Rochester on the day which followed this sleepless night: I wanted to hear his voice again, yet feared to meet his eye."

"My future was becoming to me my whole world; and more than the world; almost my hope of heaven. He stood between me and every thought of religion, as an eclipse intervenes between man and the broad sun. I could not in those days see God for His creature, of whom I had made an idol."

Charlotte Brontë was much criticized for her character Rochester and the "vulgar" and "coarse" love story with Jane. "Conduct hardly proper between a single man and a maid in her teens," one critic wrote. Another wrote that a clergyman's daughter should never have written such a shocking novel. Others felt that the "discontent" and emotion shown by the author on almost every page was unladylike and unchristian.

However, some of these readers saw Rochester's attraction. "Not an Adonis, but a Hercules in mind and body" one growled. Such "Byronic" heroes were fashionable if not exactly approved of – and Jane the teenage maid's passion for such a sexy rogue made the book a best seller.

TASK:

Pairs. Read the critical quotes above. Decide, if anything, is attractive – even loveable? – about Rochester. Remember how boring Thornfield was before he came home. Make a list of what Jane (and perhaps the reader?) loves about him. (Add any points of your own, if they're different. If you can't tell your partner, make a private list!) Does it matter that he's rude and grumpy when he speaks to her? What makes him so attractively different from John Reed, who also bullied and fought with her but whom she despised, and also from St. John, whom she says "beset" her "almost as hard" though "in a different way" from Rochester's way? Do you prefer Rochester lordly or when he's lame and half blind at the end? Does he have to be tamed by fire and injury? Why?

"Jane Eyre, who had been an ardent, expectant woman – almost a bride – was a cold solitary girl again…a Christmas frost had come at midsummer; a white December storm had whirled over June."

At the end of the book, when they are both so happy, is he still essentially the old Rochester, only NOW without the means and thus the temptation to deceive and control Jane?
Of course, there are no "right" or "wrong" answers to all these questions. Any sensible opinion that takes account of the evidence should get you credit.

BERTHA AND BLANCHE

TASK 1:

Re-read the descriptions of the Thornfield house party, especially the arrival (the "fluttering veils and waving plumes filled the air" and "rich raven ringlets" passage) and the description of Blanche's face and character ("the noble bust...black ringlets"). Jane has already drawn an anticipated likeness of the beautiful, glamorous and accomplished Blanche, and here she sees if she has been right. Has she?

TASK 2:

Design a cover for *People* magazine featuring Blanche. Make sure you capture the pride and haughtiness as well as the beauty. Don't forget the headline and tantalizing snippets of information to draw the reader in.

TASK 3:

Write a feature on the Thornfield house party and the rumors of a Rochester-Ingram "society" wedding. You will need answers to the "wh"-questions – who, when, what happened – in your first paragraph. You should start with the glamorous arrival of Mr. Rochester and Blanche on horseback, with her purple riding cloak and veil streaming on the breeze (this would make a good photo for your article). Use Jane's honest but love-struck description of Rochester's "firm grim mouth," "stern features," and "eye both brilliant and gentle." In your report bring out the way the "ugly" Rochester's character makes everyone else's beauty and elegance look trivial. (Hint: it might help if you are, like Jane, a little love-struck by him too! Lots of exclamations!)

Also include the first descent of the ladies – they descended the staircase ...as noiselessly as a bright mist rolls down a hill ("What beautiful ladies!" gasps Adèle) and some details of the party and the elegant guests.

Note- One snobbish early critic of the book said that Brontë described the ladies after dinner (from "Coffee is handed") brilliantly until they open their mouths, after which they speak in far too "common" and "vulgar" a fashion for real ladies, revealing Brontë's ignorance of such society. But celebrity ladies behaving badly (like a posh version of *Desperate Housewives*!) might be a key part of your story.

Have a scandal-sniffing feature on Adèle, Rochester's guilty secret. Who and where is the little Parisienne's mother? "Ooh la la Monsieur!" could be your headline. What is your angle - "Oh what a little puppet!" (as Blanche *pretends* to feel warmth toward her, while she later reveals her true feelings, calling Adèle a "tiresome monkey" and "a doll" she will send away to school at the first opportunity). Or will you write a sympathetic piece about how much Adèle loves dressing up as a lady, following her "earnest and innate devotion to matters of dress"?

BERTHA AND BLANCHE

TASK 4:

Red Top Scandal! Now imagine that just after finishing and sending off your "society" piece for *People*, you stumble upon the *real* scandal of Thornfield Hall: Bertha, the Mad Wife in the Attic. The other guests might be fooled by Rochester's explanation of the terrible scream in the night – and even Jane doesn't yet see past Grace Poole to the terrible truth behind the wounded Mason – but you see it all. Read Jane's descriptions of Bertha and the details of her story, including the full horror of "the maniac" with her "shaggy locks," "purple face" and "bloated" features. Contrast in size and character the clear-eyed Jane with the "demon," the "fierce ragout" in all her corpulent bulk who grabs Rochester's throat and tries to bite him! Make a contrast in your feature between Bertha and the governess, to whom only you have noticed Rochester seems to give more real attention than his supposed fiancee. But if you're really good you'll be able to compare Bertha with Blanche: both are big, attractive, Spanish-dark, glamorous, fortune-hunting women, except that all Bertha's (Creole) beauty and pride is now in ruins.
What a story this is! This is bigger than *People*. This is good enough for the front page of *The Enquirer*.
You can make your career in journalism with this – if you're brave enough.

MRS. FAIRFAX, GRACE POOLE, ADÈLE, SOPHIE

TASK 1:

Skimming/research: using the Thornfield section of the novel, skim for references to one of the following female characters: MRS. FAIRFAX, GRACE POOLE, ADÈLE, or SOPHIE. Underline and mark important information. These minor characters have all been praised for being "well drawn" and therefore giving a greater sense of reality to the whole story.

TASK 2:

Using your skimmed pages and references, describe what part your chosen character plays in the novel. In pairs, quiz your character about themselves, their job at Thornfield, their daily dealings with Jane and what they think of her, and what they know about the "Mad Wife In the Attic".

STRUCTURE AND PLOT

Jane Eyre is a very carefully constructed text. The storyline, for example, is constructed in five sections.

1. **Gateshead**
2. **Lowood**
3. **Thornfield**
4. **Moor House**
5. **Ferndean**

The novel is in effect an adventure story, a quest, or even a pilgrimage. (Or a board game!) Each section represents a stage in the personal journey of Jane's life from misery, rage and loneliness to happiness, contentment and love. She learns vital lessons at each stage, and while we tend to be on her side throughout, she is not always right. She faces – and suffers because of - her own faults and the harshness of others. But she earns her happy ending, and her sincerity and potential for real love and happiness are present from the start. We learn with her, sharing her faulty perceptions as well as her revelations.

TASK:

Think of a symbol for each section of the story – perhaps one drawn from the story itself, e.g. a mad wife in the attic for Thornfield. Sketch these symbols onto a separate sheet. Then think carefully about a color or color combination that suits the mood of each section. (Does your color come from the section itself, e.g. red and white for angry/ghostly Gateshead, river blue for Moor House? Color in your symbol.)

Plot

The events of *Jane Eyre* – every single thing that happens in Jane's autobiography - are called the "storyline." But the five-part division above is part of what is called the plot. A plot is how a storyline is shaped.

Some editions of *Jane Eyre* (following the Victorian "three decker" structure) add a further plot device, the division of the book into three volumes: volume one covers Gateshead, Lowood and half of Thornfield, two begins in the middle of Thornfield after Jane saves Rochester from the fire, and three begins near the end of Thornfield, with the discovery of the marriage, and then covers Moor House and Ferndean.

TASK 1:

Do you think these cross divisions would help?

Would they make the book easier to understand or follow? Why / why not?

TASK 2:

You are a publisher intending to bring out a new edition of *Jane Eyre* online. You are going to break it down into twelve monthly parts to help online reading. Where will you put your divisions?

The word "plot" began in Elizabethan drama as a word for the list of frantic costume and scene changes that stagehands and actors followed behind the scenes. The plot of a novel is closely connected to the storyline, but includes the way an author shapes it. For example, the plot of *Jane Eyre* is the storyline plus its arrangement - as in the device by which eight years are concentrated into one chapter (five) after four chapters have described only three months in Jane's tenth year. It would also include the device of flashbacks or forwards if there were any. It does include all the storylines – for example Rochester's past, Adèle's history, Bertha's life in the West Indies – as woven in to Jane's autobiography, often in a highly concentrated form. The plot is what happens in the book, in the order they happen, rather than the order they may have happened in real life. It is the way the author makes us share Jane's story, sometimes in unexpected, exciting – or even deliberately frustrating – ways, as in cliff hangers and disappointments (the interrupted wedding) and in foreshadowing of these (as in the chestnut tree blasted by a thunderbolt). It is also – vitally – the way the author makes us see the storyline, often in terms of contrasts, conflicts and twists.

STRUCTURE AND PLOT

TASK:

Below is a checklist for plot. You can use it for any novel. Test it out now on *Jane Eyre*.

(a) What happens?
(b) What's the chronology – in what order do the events narrated happen in real time - and how is this order presented in the story?
(c) What is the climax – if there is one - and how does the story build to it? What are the complications?
(d) Is there a central problem or conflict that drives the plot? What is it?
(e) Is it resolved and, if so, how?

One crucial function of the plot and storyline (as well as the narrative and language patterning) of *Jane Eyre* is that Brontë makes us continually compare and judge characters against each other. This is often achieved by presenting the characters in a paired (binary opposition) or three-way comparison and contrast. For example, Jane's story is structured so that we read about her overpowering marriage proposal from St. John with the overpowering one from Rochester still in our minds, and she even points out the comparison and contrast ("as hard beset by him now as I had been once before, in a different way, by another"). The plot is deliberately pulling the threads of two story lines together here. This makes us think about the relative values of the two characters – and it is just before Jane makes her final choice.

TASK 1:

What positive and negative values of the two characters – drawn together by this technique – are highlighted here? What is the key difference that makes us prefer Rochester?

TASK 2:

Another example is the way each stage of the story is made to reflect – as well as develop – an earlier stage. Or, to put it another way, the early stage is made to foreshadow the later. Think about the way Jane is shown in the red room very early on and the way Rochester reports that Bertha was put in the attic many years later, quite late in the book. How does this fit the way these events occurred in real time?

RE-PLOTTING *JANE EYRE* FOR HOLLYWOOD

TASK:

Groups. You have been asked to adapt *Jane Eyre* for TV or Hollywood. You decide you want to jazz things up a bit with flashbacks, flash forwards, parallel stories cut into each other, etc. You start it with the married Jane in Ferndean, telling the story to her own children…

Plan your re-plotting of the story. (But you must not change the actual story.) Remember to have cliffhangers, especially if it's for a series of TV episodes. And if it's for a film, you might like to experiment with the following filmic template:

a. We meet the main characters and the situation. Everything is settled and everyone knows where they are. (Equilibrium can be quite a long stage, but needs vague and growing sense of (b) or it will get boring.)

b. Something or someone comes along and unsettles everything (displacement – this can go on for most of the film).

c. It all finally sorts itself out (resolution.)

d. There is a new settled situation, with everything and everyone in a different and (in *Jane Eyre*) better place than at first. (New equilibrium – "they all lived happily ever after" – except St. John, who died happily ever after?)

WORKSHEET

The Plot Thickens Even Further!

Hollywood likes your adaptation plan, but before you start filming they have asked you to restructure Charlotte Brontë's plot to highlight connections between the following:

TASKS 1–3:

1. They want you to compare Helen Burns and St. John Rivers – and they want to film both characters next to a winter river on the snow-covered Yorkshire moors. You tell them Brontë's storyline kept the characters hundreds of pages apart (except for one reference when Jane returns to Gateshead half way through the Thornfield segment) but they tell you the water and cold are character comparisons and they want them in adjacent frames. How will you replot the story?

2. Your point about Helen Burns being mentioned by Jane at Aunt Reed's deathbed when Jane goes back to Gateshead has given them an idea. They want you to replot your film so that the entire film starts there. They say you can flashback from present Gateshead (with the grown up Georgiana and Eliza) to Gateshead and Lowood and early Thornfield from there, and then Jane can go back to Thornfield once Aunt Reed has died. You're furious because you've already started filming, but they say you can just re-order the frames to fit.

3 A Jamaican director takes over and wants more of Bertha's point of view. He wants to shoot the scene where Jane is cold and "standing in a pool," having just saved Rochester from a fiery deathbed. The director has a brilliant close up in the can of the actor playing Rochester with that "strange energy…in his voice; strange fire in his look" and a great response shot of Jane trying to get away from him. But he now wants you to write a sequence in which Bertha watches them from the shadows in her chains. We don't see her, but we get her angle on the frame of Jane and Rochester, and we hear her growls and snarls. She can mutter her response to their actions – remember she has just tried to incinerate Rochester in his bed and will clasp him in a deathly embrace next time she sees him. But she does not harm Jane even when she has the chance, only tears the bridal veil. Write the sequence, with Bertha's speech below each frame. Finally, the director – who thinks the book is about the enslavement of women - wants you to make a link between Bertha chained to chair in the attic and Jane in the red room (where, like Bertha, she is described as a "mad cat") and on the chair in Lowood. Restructure your plot to bring these three stories together.

NARRATIVE

Perhaps the most powerful influence in the plotting of any storyline is who tells the story. In fact, so powerful is this aspect of "plot" that it has a separate category of its own: Narrative.

TASK 1:

"Unjust- unjust!" In pairs, tell your partner about a childhood incident where you recall another child – a sibling perhaps – wronging you in some way.

(a) Did an adult arbitrate?

(b) Were you supported, or was the adult "unjust"?

TASK 2:

Now the hard bit. Try – honestly and accurately, as if it is someone else involved – telling the story of the incident from the other child's point of view. Make a note of

(a) factual differences, if any, and

(b) a difference in how the story "comes across" even if it's the same facts.

Did You Know? The author Jean Rhys actually rewrote the whole of *Jane Eyre* from Bertha's point of view in a book called *Wide Sargasso Sea*. The book focuses on Bertha's life in the West Indies and the circumstances in which she married Rochester. It emphasises how Bertha's "Creole" (mixed race) background and the context of the slave trade may make us read the chaining up of what Brontë calls a "savage" in the dark with sympathy and outrage as much as horror.

TASK 3:

Can you find evidence of Bertha's Creole background possibly being used as a shock device for Brontë's mainly white Victorian readers?

NARRATIVE

WORKSHEET 1

The Biography of an Auto

Our book *Jane Eyre* is described as an autobiography. This is intriguing because an autobiography (auto = self) is usually non-fiction, and indeed some readers confuse the events of Brontë's own life (there are some similarities) with those of her completely made up character, Jane. But a fictional character can't have an autobiography because she doesn't even have a biography.

This is another function of the narrative – who is telling it? We are told in *Jane Eyre* that we are reading someone's life story. It is the narrative of an older – secure, happily married woman – looking back over a traumatic life. She begins her last chapter, "Reader, I married him." So it is clearly meant to be like an autobiography. But Jane refers more than once to what she is writing as a novel, a fiction, as if any life story is a fiction in any case.

The fact that "Jane" is telling the story looking back is a kind of ongoing flashback. There are many passages where the younger Jane relives passion and trouble as if it is still present. But equally, the adult narrator is guiding us through an adult analysis of mistakes as well as satisfactions.

TASK:

Think back to any incident in your life where you are ashamed at what you did then and now think you know better. Jot down the details, saying how you learned to deal with it in a different way. Are there any mistakes you've made that you think you will make again? Any powerful experiences where you are very proud of how you handled it? Finally, any mistakes where your reaction may not have been perfect but did include some qualities you're still proud of?

WORKSHEET 2

Jane's Autobiography

TASK:

Pick one of the following episodes in Jane's life and try to distinguish between what the young Jane felt and did at the time from what the later adult Jane might judge to be good or bad. Are there any moments she is proud of? Any mixed feelings – of pride and shame at what she did?

1. Her rage at John ("a picture of passion") and its aftermath in the red room ("embers of my decaying ire")
2. Her love-driven jealousy about Blanche's beauty as anticipated by Mrs. Fairfax: "Tall, fine bust, sloping shoulders; long, graceful neck, olive complexion …eyes ...brilliant as her jewels." Also the way Jane tries to deal with it at the time by her two sketches of herself and the imagined Blanche on the last page of chapter sixteen. Remember that when Jane is writing this she is Rochester's wife; when she was living it, such a thing seemed impossible.
3. Her rejection of Rochester. ("Gentle reader, may you never feel what I felt then… never shed such stormy, scalding, heart-rung tears," an acute distress revisited later about surrendering to temptation.)
4. Her last-minute rejection of the apparently omnipotent St. John. Does she manage this, or was it managed for her? Is there any difference between how she understood this at the time compared to the adult Jane looking back? Compare "'Down superstition!' I commented, as that spectre rose up black by the black yew at the gate…this is not witchcraft…" to the analysis of a secure and settled woman looking back saying, "It was my time to assume ascendancy." Is that how she felt at the time?

WORD PATTERNS IN *JANE EYRE*

You may already have noticed that the plot links are supported by other links, like names and language. Reeds are found near rivers. St. John (Rivers) is a much more saintly person than John (Reed), and we see a genuine Christian in his taking in of a stranger. But - as the foreshadowing might have warned us – he is no less a bully than the first John in the end. The whole plot emphasises this – the whole novel and its story of Jane's trials pretty much starts with John Reed, and it certainly ends with St. John. But the names are a crucial support for this patterning.

TASK 1:

Name patterns are a major part of the book. In groups, jot down any names you have noticed that make references to the English Civil War and especially to fire and water.

TASK 2:

The fire and water patterns are not restricted to names. What general language patterns can you find of a fire/water opposition? What is the significance of fire/heat and water/coldness in terms of characters and their actions?

TASK 3:

Now look for the religious names in the novel. What do these names suggest about the characters who bear them? Then –and only then- check the Brontë biographies and timelines for any reasons why religion might be important to the author. Does this add to our understanding, or is Brontë's experience of religion too different from Jane's to be suggestive?

TASK 4:

Now think about the language of heat and cold and religion together. Jane and Rochester finally achieve human warmth in their married love at sheltered woody Ferndean. They are no longer "out in the cold" of loneliness, but they are no longer in danger of turning their home into a "hell" of unmarried and unbridled passion, either. They have balanced heat and cold. For contrast, where do St. John and Helen Burns – whose religious names combine heat and water- and the fiery Bertha end up?

ADVANCED STRUCTURAL PATTERNS

Brontë often matches one opposite with another and then strikes a balance that goes beyond both extremes. Rochester goes beyond Bertha's fire. Jane goes beyond St. John's ice. They come back to each other somewhere in the middle.

There are many patterns like this in the novel. They go deeper than simple names and words, though they are often indicated by them. The whole structure of the book throws up patterns, comparisons and contrasts.

TASK:

In pairs, study the list of patterns given in the table below. Pick one to research. Look up examples from the relevant sections of the novel. Try to explain or at least explore how the pattern may work (e.g. opposites or extremes overcome - or put together to make a larger third? Or just compared?) Present a short relevant passage from the book as a reading to a group and discuss your findings and analysis of patterns with the group or to the whole class.

Patterns	**Patterns**	**Comments**
"Ugly" Rochester and "plain" Jane ("Servants...never saw anybody so much in love as he was... he was after her continually") (consummated)	St. John (handsome as a Greek god) and Rosamond (literally "rose of the world") (i.e. very beautiful) (denied)	Both couples are physically and personally compatible and really love each other. There is a further pattern in the R and J (like Romeo and Juliet) of their names. The ugly ones marry!
Domineering males, John Reed and then Brocklehurst, both try to control Jane, but fail.	Domineering male St. John controls Jane - almost hypnotizes her – but fails at the very last.	Rochester by contrast is Jane's "master" - *but only when what he asks her to do is right (in her eyes).*
Neither logic nor passion. Hard. Cold. Black pillar. Like a gravestone?	Reason without feeling. Hard. Cold. White marble. In love with death.	Bertha is passion without logic - and Rochester is passion beyond logic. Taught by Jane, and purged by fire, the "Ferndean" Rochester blends both.
Black stone	White marble: "Inexorable priest, yet the man is not tranquil. A statue of snow, and fire burns beneath. But the fire will not thaw the ice." (Skelton, *Fraser's Magazine* 1857)	Fire
Helen Burns – death through love?	St. John – death over love?	Rochester and Jane – love until death.
Water: Helen Burns, Grace Poole, St. John Rivers, the Reeds, ice at Lowood, snow at Morton, the mountain river St. John proposes by.	Fire: The red room, Helen Burns, singeing Rivers, Bertha's pyromania, the Indian sun, the practice of suttee (= Jane's marriage to St. John), the thunderbolt in the chestnut tree, human warmth and firesides (Bessie, Moor House).	Fire and water are opposites and represent important themes in the novel. Water associated with dousing or damping down of passion or of excitement. (Grace Poole a comically dull character; Bertha is wild excitement personified: Jane crucially – and comically- mistakes one for the other for most of her time at Thornfield.)
Rose (Rosamond = rose of the world) – symbol of romance and beauty.	Thorn – ugly and painful. Not many of these in pretty Rosamond's life, or Blanche Ingram's? – or in the kind of love stories they read – or might write - or might imagine themselves in? They both give up at the first sign of trouble.	Jane has a thorny and very prickly time at Thornfield, but it is where her love and romance – her "home" - is found. She does not give up until she finds it, even when Thornfield itself has burnt down.

ADVANCED STRUCTURAL PATTERNS IN *JANE EYRE*

Patterns	Patterns	Comments
Charades – Rochester and Blanche's charade portrays marriage as Bridewell (a prison). Their marriage would be a charade, just as his marriage to Bertha was and is – and just as his attempted wedding (or bigamy) to Jane is. The falsities of romance behind many a so-called "happy ending"? (Bertha's most of all?) False romance.	Real relationships: Jane offers these at every stage of her life – even in retrospect to her dying Aunt Reed, whom she would not call Aunt because of the un-aunt like treatment. She wants a family more than money and puts her money where her mouth is. She will not be Rochester's mistress, only his wife. She will not be St. John's wife, only his "sister." She is more genuinely a mother to little Adèle than her "real" mother ever was. She is professional with all her contacts, even getting a reference from Mr. Brocklehurst and fulfilling her obligations to the Reeds. Realism.	Thornfield is a charade. An aristocratic charade, the charade of an England that has gone? It has a mad wife in the attic, a mock courtship with a fortune hunter in the public rooms, a "ward" from a previous affair in the nursery/schoolroom, a concealed love affair that becomes a barely restrained engagement behind the scenes with the governess, climaxing in a near-bigamy in the church. It is burned down. From the burnt shell of this charade emerges Ferndean – a far less showy but respectable, almost middle-class reality. The triumph of realism and romance?
Jane Eyre – air, heir, eyrie. Jane, Joan, Janet – a plain name and also the female equivalent of John, of which there are several in the book, and which used to be the most common male name in England. It gives her a kind of equivalence and equality with them – fighting John, traveling dumbly with the servant John, fighting off St. John, plotting her little surprise for the blind Rochester with the servant John later. Possibly a suggestion also of "eerie" in Eyre: Jane is compared (often by Rochester) to spectres, witches, sorceresses, elves and fairies and has dreams and presentiments throughout the story.	Fire and water are the elements in which Jane's story is told. Her own name suggests "air," a third element, - free, elevated (like an eagle in her eyrie – looking down as she did from the window at Gateshead before John's violent interruption and as she often did at Thornfield, unconsciously waiting for something to happen.) Not like Bertha in the burning turrets of Thornfield, though – more perhaps like the author, she is looking back from the moral heights she's scaled.	Air also suggests "heir" – and Jane is certainly an heir to a fairy tale fortune, which gives her very real independence – though not the spiritual independence to finally refuse St. John's threatened prison. She needed love – and Rochester – for that. But is the "heir" symbolic as well? What else is she "heir" to beyond the fortune her Aunt cheated her of? Heir to the world maybe, and all it offers, including a loving marriage – just as any John Heir would be – no longer any less so for being a woman? Though this was in many ways still a dream for women in 1847, it is a dream this book, among others, helped to put on the map of possibility – made it a realistic aim.
Mrs. Reed and the two Reed sisters. The worldly, cold-hearted parent of conventionally attractive daughters: Jane by contrast has no mother or father and is not conventionally attractive, though she is the "magical", and non-conventional "daughter" of a ghost (her Uncle John) and then of a sort of fairy godfather in Madeira (another Uncle John).	The pattern continues and repeats: (1) The cold, worldly Brocklehurst (a pillar) and the two Brocklehurst sisters. (2) The cold, worldly Lady Ingram (with a pillar throat) and the two Ingram sisters.	The pattern develops: St. John qualifies as the equivalent of the cold "pillar" parent in some ways – "at the fireside… a cold cumbrous column, gloomy and out of place." But he is not worldly, and the two (now parentless and orphaned) Rivers sisters are loving and warm.

IMAGERY

1. **In groups, and using the language patterns grids as well as the patterns and ideas in the novel, create a mind map** (see page 67) of all the names, words and phrases you can think of to do with fire/warmth/passion/red contrasted with those to do with water/coldness/self-control/white. (E.g. Jane is standing in a pool after saving Rochester from fire, Bertha – fire, Rochester "strange fire in his look", Grace Poole – jailer, St. John Rivers. Where will you put Helen Burns? Blanche Ingram? The West Indies is steamy and hot – but so is Thornfield – "Italian days" around the time of Rochester's proposal – and so is "missionary" India.) Include any characters that are associated with stone in your cold category. Do some places seem colder and more wintry than others in the book? (E.g. Lowood compared with Thornfield?)

2. **Decide if fire and red and heat, etc., are ever all positive - and if white and cold and wet are ever all negative, or are both always mixed?** Why are both St. John the missionary and Bertha the mad wife both associated with hot countries? Or is St. John's spiritual fire really cold, even in India? Is Miss Temple right to be marble-cold when faced with Brocklehurst's fervor? Is any character ever the "right" blend of fire and cold?

3. Brontë is a very moral writer, and her character Jane resists every temptation to give in to her overpowering love for Rochester, though not without a very human struggle. We are not so moral as the Victorians about such things. Despite this, in her own day, Brontë was criticized for her heroine choosing the warm, "reformed rake" Rochester to the cold and/or holy-burning St. John. **Does anyone in your group think Jane should have chosen St. John? Does anyone think Jane should never have left Thornfield for her long-suffering "journey into asceticism with St. John"?**

4. **THINK: What does Jane gain from leaving Thornfield for the wilderness of the moors and Morton?** Tick the box to say whether you agree or disagree. You need to have reasons for your answers. Tick twice for strong feelings. Is the group's overall view that Jane should have simply accepted Rochester because they loved each other?

Statement	Agree	Disagree
Jane and Rochester were made for each other, and Jane leaving merely tortures them both for no reason.		
Jane's stubbornness indirectly causes Rochester's fire injuries.		
Jane indirectly causes Bertha's death.		
Jane only flees Thornfield because she cares what society thinks.		
By refusing Rochester's offer of "living in sin" after his exposure as a bigamist, Jane gains equality in marriage.		
Rochester might have tired of Jane – just as he tired of his earlier mistresses.		
Rochester needs to suffer to appreciate Jane when he does finally get her.		
Rochester was treating Jane as a sort of doll during their engagement; he needed to learn to see her as an equal.		

IMAGERY

Statement	Agree	Disagree
Jane already deserved Rochester after refusing his advances until he proposed – she does not deserve the torments she had with St. John, and they teach her nothing.		
From her time with St. John, the "little nun" Jane learns to value human love and passion as well as – and in the end more than - Lowood duty.		
Jane strings St. John along – she should have come clean about Rochester.		
Jane becomes a successful teacher in Morton, gaining a very real independence not many Victorian women had.		
The "sound English education" she achieves for her Morton girls helps her later as a parent choosing the right school for "little Adèle." Correcting her "French defects" but not too strict – though not too indulgent either.		

JANE EYRE AND WORD PAINTING

Charlotte Brontë herself was often described as a "painter" with words, and she tends to represent characters and incidents in the way an original visual artist of that period might.

Early critics talked of Brontë as if she was a painter. *The Christian Remembrancer* wrote in April 1848, "she has a painter's eye and hand." Now read this early critical response to *Jane Eyre* by G.H. Lewes (published in *Fraser's Magazine*, December 1847).

"The characters are few, and drawn with unusual mastery: even those that are but sketched – such as Mr. Brocklehurst, Miss Temple, Mrs. Fairfax, Rosamond, and Blanche – are sketched with a vividness which betrays the cunning hand: a few strokes, and the figure rises before you...
Mr. Rochester is also well drawn, and from the life; but it is a portrait of a man drawn by a woman, and is not comparable to the portrait of Jane... there is both art and artifice (in the handling of St. John Rivers, the missionary) and, although true in the main, and very powerful in parts, one feels a certain misgiving about him: it is another example of the woman's pencil...
The story is so simple in its outlines yet so filled out – not spun out -with details...The pictures stand out distinctly before you: they are pictures"
"To her we emphatically say...keep reality distinctly before you, and paint it as accurately as you can.."

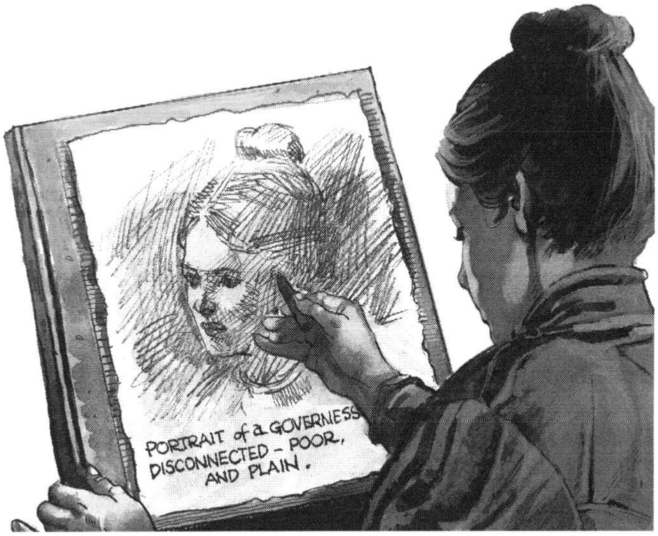

DISCUSSION: Do you agree that Brontë paints with words? Give an example.

BOOK REPORT

A book report summarizes the content of a book. Write a book report about *Jane Eyre*.

Name: ______________________

Date: ______________________

Book Title: ______________________

Author: ______________________

Artwork: ______________________

Publisher: ______________________

ISBN: ______________________

No of Pages: ______________________

Characters: Who were the main characters?

Setting: Where and when was the book set?

Plot: What happens in the book?

Did you like or dislike the book? Explain why.

What new words or facts did you learn?

Ending: What happens at the end?

BOOK REVIEW

A book review is more detailed than a book report and assesses the book's strengths and weaknesses. When writing your book review of *Jane Eyre,* think about these.
You may find some of these early reviews of *Jane Eyre* useful as a starting point. Do you agree or disagree with them?

Plain, poor and little? – "the little Jane with her sharp eyes and dogmatic speeches, is a being you neither could fondle nor love." Do you agree?

A Cinderella figure? - Jane is an orphan and a dependant in the house of a selfish, hardhearted aunt. She is thrown upon the cruelty of relations who neglect and abuse her. She becomes revengeful and superstitious and almost supernaturally threatening, and her spirit rebels instead of breaking. Then she goes to Lowood, (a girls' equivalent of the many boys' schools in other Victorian novels like Dickens' *Nicholas Nickleby*), where she contrives to enlist our sympathies for a time with her little pinched fingers, cropped hair and empty stomach...

She learns – in wretched conditions - **patience and principle** rather than passion.

Adèle is **"childhood naturally depicted"**. A superb character. Do you agree?

Girls' education was becoming an important issue. Some Victorian writers believed girls should be taught to be kind and sweet to their husbands rather than study arithmetic: more radical thinkers insisted that equal education could liberate women. *Jane Eyre* is very concerned with this question. Bored of teaching, Jane becomes the **governess** of an opera dancer's illegitimate daughter. Frivolous, pretty and pampered, Adèle is the opposite of Jane except that she's also an orphan, and at Jane's hands she learns *some* Lowood strictness. Is Adèle (and Georgiana, and Blanche and others) a reverse mirror for Lowood Jane? – An example of what a girl may become if pampered rather than brought up along Lowood lines? Or is the message that neither kind of extreme upbringing is right? (Check with how Jane arranges Adèle's education at the end of the novel.)

In the end, the **honesty, kindness of heart, and perseverance** of the heroine, are seen as **triumphant over every obstacle**. Is this a good description of the overall purpose and message of the book?

Passion for a rogue? – "the reader cannot see anything loveable in Mr. R, nor why he should be so deeply in love with Jane Eyre." Can you?

Read the passage where Jane observes the fine ladies. One critic says their descent from table is exquisite but that the vulgar sniping she then overhears is implausible talk for a lady. A lady shouldn't talk like this, certainly, but what do you think? Do ladies always talk how they should?

TASK:

The love story was said to represent **"conduct hardly proper"** between a single man and a maid in her teens. **What do you think?**

BOOK REVIEW

A book review is more detailed than a book report and assesses the book's strengths and weaknesses. When writing your review of *Jane Eyre* think about these: Did you find the book interesting?
Did the format of the book help you to understand what was happening?
What was your reaction to the story?
Did you learn anything?
What would you have done differently to Charlotte Brontë?
Would you recommend this book to others?
Continue on a separate sheet if you need to.

Book Title: ______________________
Author: ______________________
Artwork: ______________________
Publisher: ______________________
ISBN: ______________________
No of Pages: ______________________

Once your book review is finished you could upload it to one of the many book review websites such as:

www.amazon.com
www.whosreadit.com
www.kidsreview.org.uk
www.mrsmad.com
www.teensreadtoo.com
www.teenspoint.org

Book Review:

____

Name: ______________________
Date: ______________________

CHARACTER AND MOTIVATION

Here we explore links and relationships between the key characters, although the mind map can be used in many ways to explore other themes within the novel, such as motivation.

TASK:

Draw a mind map linking Jane, Bertha, Blanche and Rochester.
Is it love, hate or passion linking them…or all three…or something else?

Below is an example of a mind map.

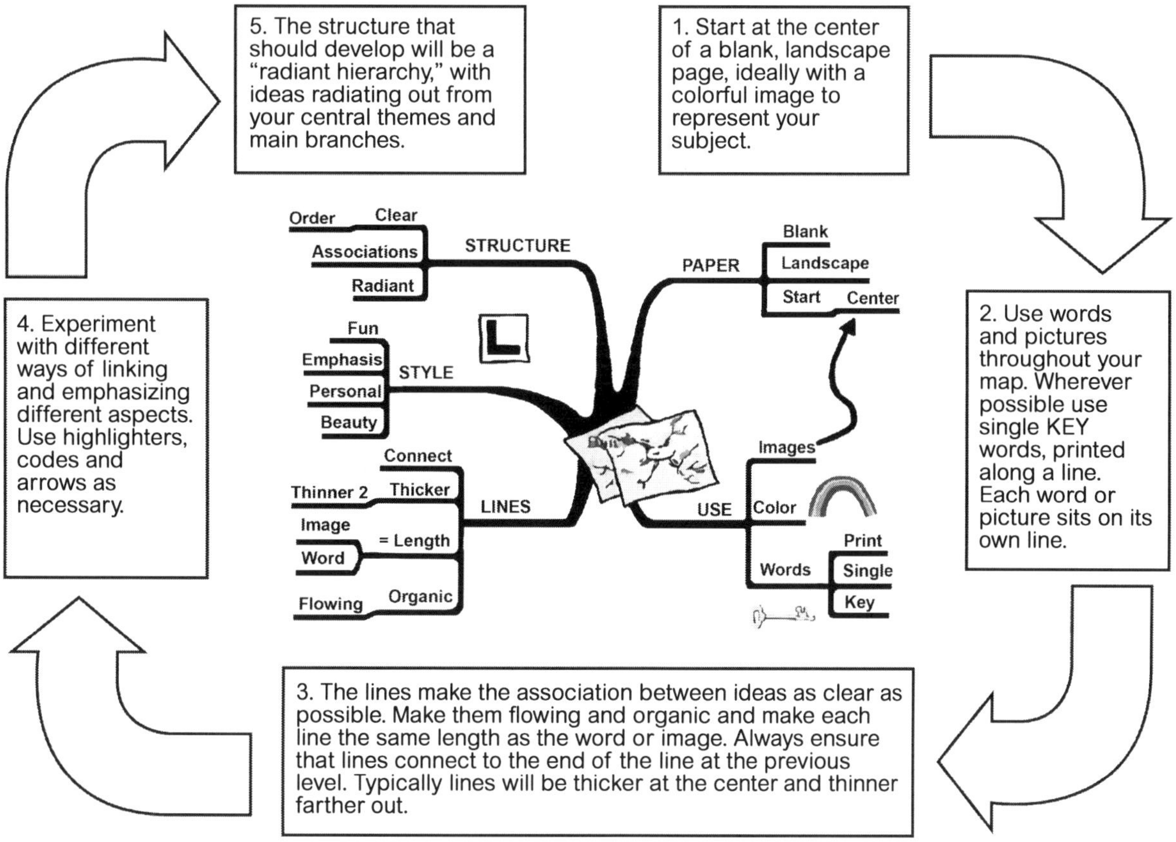

Use one of the images from the book in the center of the page to start you off.

Now draw lines to each character showing who is related to whom, how they are connected in other ways and any other "joining" threads you can think of.

Explain the connections, using quotes where you can.

POLICE INVESTIGATION

MAD WIFE IN ATTIC COURT CASE

Groups. Millcote Summer Murders. Four members of your group are a crack team of detectives and police officers. Two of you are journalists. Another is a Judge. Another is a defense lawyer. Another two are eyewitnesses of (a) how Bertha was "kept" and (b) her death. You are all also the court.

You will all find as much evidence from the novel as you can about Bertha Mason's *actual* crimes (Thornfield section and the report about "the lunatic wife" in the Ferndean section). One member of the group is a police officer who then assembles the group's evidence into something like the following:

Sets fire to Rochester's bed while he is asleep in it. Arson. Attempted murder?
Steals knife from her guard, with later intent to harm. Theft and malicious intent.
Bites and stabs her brother, Richard Mason, during the Ingram house party.
Destroys property (a bridal veil) belonging to Miss Eyre. Threatening behavior towards her.
Wanders the house at night – two occasions reported - with intent to commit crimes.
Assaults husband.

The police officer reads the above to the group.

An eyewitness then reads the account below:

"The lunatic sprang and grappled his throat viciously, and laid her teeth to his cheek: they struggled. She was a big woman, in stature almost equaling her husband, and corpulent besides: she showed virile force in the contest – more than once she almost throttled him, athletic as he was. He could have settled her with a well planted blow; but he would not strike; he would only wrestle."

Bertha has been murdered – or has she?

Another police officer adds the latest addition to Bertha's record. Attempted Murder, Suicide (a capital crime then) Arson, Wilful Destruction of Property: The first police officer rewrites his notes and then reads out the dramatic account of Bertha's final arson "she was on the roof…waving her arms above the battlements...a big woman…long black hair…streaming against the flames"

Give these pages to two other members of the group who represent the press. They rewrite the material as a newspaper report. Meanwhile, another member of the group rewrites it as a report to give to the court. Give this report to the court now.

You are Bertha's defense lawyer, Mr. John Rhys. She is accused of suicide and attempted murder and if convicted will not be buried in consecrated ground (therefore going to hell). It's the injustice you hate, and Rochester in your view shouldn't get away with it. Also, you knew Bertha as an unspoiled girl before she met Rochester. You are also very keen on the legal rights of women. Find as much mitigating evidence as possible from the novel – there isn't much.

POLICE INVESTIGATION

MAD WIFE IN ATTIC COURT CASE

She is his legal wife (but therefore legally Rochester's property at that time) and the presence of Blanche – whom she closely resembles in every aspect – and Jane (whom Rochester clearly loves and whose "wedding apparel" "perhaps brought back vague reminisces of her own bridal days") threatens that status and memory.

She is insane (but Rochester's home custody was a relative kindness at that time of primitive asylums like Bedlam) and so not as clearly responsible for her actions as a sane woman would be (however, lunatics did not have legal status in the modern sense).

Her "caretaker" drinks, allowing her to escape: not her fault.

You note the following from accounts of how Bertha is treated. "Fierce yells…convulsive plunges… Grace Poole gave him a cord…he bound her to a chair."

"Cunning as a witch" – regularly escapes legal custody by stealing Grace Poole's key and "roaming all about the house doing …wild mischief"

Include those details into a summary of your own.

Now give this evidence to the court.

Detective interviews with witnesses. Two of you are detectives. Read the account Rochester gives Jane of his courtship and early married life to Bertha. It is where the reader at last learns the horrifying secret of Thornfield Hall. The Bertha marriage is a sordid affair, but aristocratic marriages were traditionally based on land transactions traded off against the physical charms of the woman rather than on love - he himself draws the exact parallel with Blanche Ingram and "planter" families (with their slave-worked plantations) who had been marrying into the aristocracy for mutual gain and greed like this for a century. There was also, among the rather in-bred aristocracy, a greater than usual chance (and fear) of insanity running through the family. Brontë shows Rochester in a not uncommon situation and as behaving relatively decently – at least by the standards of that time and class. "See that she is cared for as her condition demands, and you have done all that God and Humanity require of you." Also, he clearly despises slavery, which he would have seen in his in-laws' home, Jamaica. As much as he hates the aristocratic practice of taking mistresses – "hiring a mistress is the next worst thing to buying a slave." In this respect, he is better than many of his peers.

Underline all the negative nouns and adjectives and verbs Rochester uses to describe Bertha.
(E.g. monster, "wild beast" "lunatic" "cunning" "malignant" "goblin"; elsewhere - hideous, degrading, intemperate, unchaste, pigmy intellect, giant propensities, fury, and compare with the verb "spring" as used by the servant). They are obsessively disgusting and disgusted. But Rochester is trying to persuade Jane to agree with him that he was justified in hiding Bertha away and seeking a real marriage-companion.

Discuss who you think is most to blame in the whole sordid affair.
Weigh up the facts of Bertha v Rochester. Will you now arrest Rochester – or let sleeping dogs lie?
Give your case, with analysis of the arguments, to the court.

CAN I GET A WITNESS?

TASK:

You are a witness to the death of Bertha. The judge at the Bertha Mason trial is checking the version he's heard from Rochester. Bertha's lawyer is trying to clear her of all blame in order that her family can claim life insurance and save her soul and good name. You are telling the truth as you saw it. Make up a dialog of question and answer based on the events depicted in the novel. The opening has been done for you.

Judge: "Then Mr. Rochester was at home when the fire broke out?"

Witness: "Yes."

Judge: "And he made no effort to save Mrs. Rochester?"

Witness: "No. I mean, yes, of course he did. He always cared for her."

When you've sketched out some questions and answers, improvise the scene in court.

The Judge now brings evidence from "outside" the novel. Evidence from "outside" the novel may be "inferred" from the time line of women's emancipation, notably the information about the very limited legal rights of wives (Rochester could have legally whipped Bertha until 1820) and the business and marital arrangement by which Rochester was linked to "Mr. Mason, a West India planter and merchant," whose slave workers would not have been legally freed until 1833 (effectively 1843 in reality). Both as a wife and a Creole, even a sane Bertha would have semi-captive status in Rochester's society. Perhaps, like Jane, Bertha resists this status as "unjust". Not long after Bertha went into the Thornfield attic, Jane went into the Gateshead red room – about ten years before they meet. They have much in common.

The Judge now instructs the jury in this "wider" evidence and the laws of the time.

Now the jury (all of you as a group) have to decide (a) whether Bertha Mason is guilty or innocent of all or any charges and (b) whether Rochester has anything to answer for. The group now discusses the case and delivers its verdict. Verdicts are supposed to be unanimous – this makes them more secure against appeal – but if not, there has to be a majority verdict.

Groups report their verdicts to the class as a whole.

Pairs. You are a pair of journalists in the court. Newspaper or TV. Give a detailed report of the Mad Wife On The Roof where Bertha's final arson and death fall is heard in court. Perhaps call it A VIEW TO A KILL. Read the description again. **Make a "photograph"** – by drawing it or as a tableau using the group – and/or storyboard of the description, depending on whether you are newspaper or TV.

BLUEBEARD'S WIVES

In groups, quiz the women Rochester has known before coming home to Thornfield.
You should know Bertha and Blanche Ingram well by now. Céline is described in some detail. The others and Rochester's search for a partner are briefly described on pages 88 and 89 of the graphic novel. Each member of the group plays one of these women. Try to bring out what each of these women lacks that Rochester sees and loves in Jane. For example, do you think Rochester is ugly? So, Bertha might growl, looks? "Pah! - I liked to scratch and bite him and taste his blood." (Most of what you ask her will come back to violence or triviality or both at once.) Céline might say, "'e was 'ideous, but zen ze only thing I wanted from 'im was money." Blanche might say with sarcasm – "Oh, Edward's an absolute Adonis darling. If you add on his money. Haw haw haw." The Italian beauty Giacinta might say, "you mention that brute to me again, I keel you…unless – he has gift for me? Ah! Molte bene! Come here, amore, sit on my knee." The German beauty Clara might say, "Ach, I do not know about zat. All I know is, we haf to be at zer chapel at half past nine for ze long speech about duty and still ze carriage hass not come!"

THE BERTHA MASON CASE

TASK 1:

The Bertha Mason case goes to the House of Commons as a test case. The motion is "A wife is for life, in sickness, for worse, for poorer, and not just for the husband's comfort." There are very strong arguments for divorce and remarriage – notably that Bertha seems to be criminally insane, that Rochester was "tricked" into it and that he is sincere about finding a "real" wife now that he's mature enough. But there are – and even then, were – arguments for a wife's rights too. Write your own view of the matter, based on your knowledge of Bertha's story. At the end, vote on the motion. Don't just vote for your "own" side – listen to the arguments and vote for what you then believe.

MUSIC

TASK 1:

The "blues" was music made by slaves on the boats and plantations to relieve their feelings and keep their energy going. It is no exaggeration to say that its outpouring of pain and woe maybe kept some of them alive both spiritually and physically in death camp conditions. Bertha would have lived around the time and place that blues music was first being performed.
Use a basic twelve-bar blues riff as a backing for a song called *Bertha's Blues: the View From The Attic*. See how many verses your group can compose. Something like this perhaps?

"Well I woke up this morning, chains on my wrists and legs.
Say I woke up this morning, chains on my wrists and legs.
My bridal room is an attic tomb and my husband hates the female sex."

Alternatively, you can update the blues to its modern equivalents rap or R&B. Or give it a Jamaican twist into reggae, rock steady or ska.

TASK 2:

Now perform your song!

ART

TASK 1:

Try making the description below into a sketch or painting.

"Folds of scarlet drapery shut in my view to the right hand; to the left were the clear planes of glass protecting, but not separating me from the drear November day. At intervals, while turning over the leaves of my book, I studied the aspect of that winter afternoon. Afar, it offered a pale blank of mist and cloud: near, a scene of wet lawn and storm beat shrub, with ceaseless rain sweeping away wildly before a long and lamentable blast."

TASK 2:

Choose one of Jane's three rather haunted watercolors from chapter thirteen for the same purpose.

TASK 3:

Make a sketch of the great horse chestnut tree in chapter twenty-three before and after the thunderbolt. Color in the difference between the tree on Midsummer Eve and the next day's scene of half burnt destruction.

JANE EYRE WORD SEARCH

The following words are hidden in the grid below. How many times does each word appear?

LOWOOD	RED ROOM	BERTHA	PILOT
ROCHESTER	HORSE	FIRE	WIFE
HELEN BURNS	BLANCHE	JANE EYRE	GHOST
RIVERS	JOHN REED	LOVE	ATTIC
ORPHAN	MAD	BRONTE	THORNFIELD

D R L O V E L O V E J O H N R E E D T R
A H T R E B R I V E R S B R O N T E S S
N M R E T S E H C O R F I R E R N T O E
H O R S E S N R U B N E L E H A R N H H
B O O F B E R T H A E S R O H D E O G V
L R N S R E V I R E D R P P E E I R E H
A D W I F E A D A M E L R R R L F B F P
N E S R O H A T T I C O E E I O O I I S
C R T E T M S R E V I R R I F D A M W A
H A B R M H W R T D E I O T F O A M E D
E E E I S A I I E O F T D R P N H M F D
A B R F A F D E F M L R N O P I R G I E
T E T N F I R E D E A I I O O H L O W N
T S H J A N E E Y R E D P V R W A O H E
I R A I H I E S R O H O R S E B O N T T
C O I O P R E R Y E E N A J C R C L H E
T H J V N D L E I F N R O H T E S R O H
D S H H E V L H E L E N B U R N S H R R
A J O H N R E E D H E L E N B U R N S E
M J E H E L S H G O E C P C N D O O E E

JANE EYRE WORD SEARCH

Not for beginners! The following words – all of which appear in *Jane Eyre* – are hidden in the grid below. How many times does each word appear?

RED ROOM	SCORN	JOHN REED	HELEN BURNS
BLANCHE	MADEIRA	GEORGIANA	FERNDEAN
GOVERNESS	THORNFIELD HALL	RIVERS	CLERGYMAN
TYPHUS	MAGISTRATE	CHARADES	LOWOOD
CANDLESTICK	MISSIONARY	ROCHESTER	BRONTE

I D E E R N H O J T Y P H U S C M A M A R I V E I L
N I T L O W O O D S U H P Y T H S O N A R I V I R S
O A D O O W O L B L A N C H E A S U O A D I V R N N
R E T S E H C O R E D R O O M R R C H R I E E E N H
B R Y R A N O I S S I M R E L A E I O P D G I D R S
S S S S E N R E V O G E D A M D V A A O Y E R R A S
U M A G I S T R A T E L M A D E I O B P T T R O A M
H R E S N R I V E R S H M O E S R N A A N C N R E R
P H A U O J O H N R E E D N O H R S R A E S I S H G
Y A R H C A N D E L S T I C K O U T E T N E R S E I
T R I P T Y P H U S S I R R C H S D N R D E E T Y H
C A E Y M N D S B A E S M S P I N O U A V B A R L H
V H D T E A O R R N N S C Y G R R B M I I R A L O E
N C A E T R O E O A R E T A E B N D R N T N N O W M
C R M R N I W V N I E N M F O E O E A S O R N W O H
A U O E A E O I T G V R A T L O T E I I O L N O O D
N K E S R D L R E R O E C E W N D G S C O C N O D A
D C N K B A E E K O G V H O O N A S S M O O R D E R
E I A C E M M S C E S O L R R M I R E T S E H C O R
L T S I S L I E I G R G B E T M A C L E R G Y M A N
S S N T T K S N T E J N F Y R A N O I S S I M A L U
T L A S T C S C S C L E R G Y M A N E D N S E D O O
I E E L H I I H L R B L A N C H E L T Y D T N E A R
C D D E O T O A E H C N A L B I L E N O N T T I Y G
K N N D R S N R D I S E D A R A H C O O S N H R E K
L A R N N L A A N R G E S I H N H W R B O C A A T T
G C E A F E R D A O H S D D A G O B B R R L E R N R
R S F C I D Y E C C N O L L A L L T B S D O O W O L
E E G B E N L S N R O E B F E R N D E A N Y N O R A
T W S L L A K A U W I C L E R G Y M A N U Y A T B O
S N E A D C L B O F E M L E T A R T S I G A M R E A
E A D N H B N L N B S N R U B N E L E H S C O R N O
H E A C A E N R C C O G O V E R N E S S S C O R N E
C D R H L D O S C O R N V T R I V E R S C O N R E I
O N A E L H R E T S E H C O R E L E D O O W O L E D
R R H D T G A R I E D A M R R E D R O O M C N A L B
O E C B L A N C H E T N O R B R O N T E S R E V I R
G F I M G E I A D T L A S A C I I A I O S I F L G C

JANE EYRE CROSSWORD

Complete the crossword puzzle.

Across

2 The name John Reed often called Jane (4)
3 The name of the small island where Jane's Uncle John moved to and died (7)
6 This ruined Thornfield Hall (4)
10 Home of Mrs. Reed (9)
11 Eliza's vocation (3)
16 Owner of Thornfield Hall (9)
17 The century in which Jane Eyre is set (10)
18 Mr. Rochester's dog (5)
19 A deadly infectious disease (6)
20 Rochester's secret visitor from Jamaica (5)
23 Adele lived in this country (6)
24 Where Bertha Mason is kept (5)
25 Rochester in disguise (5)
26 He created the artwork for Classical Comics graphic novel version of *Jane Eyre* (4,1,5)
29 Jane was locked in here as punishment for striking Master Reed (3,4)
31 The name of the school for orphans, where Jane is first sent (5)

Down

1 The name of Jane's role, as teacher of Adèle (9)
4 *Jane Eyre* is written in this style of book (13)
5 Daughter of Lord and Lady Ingram (7)
7 Jane's school friend (5,5)
8 The author of *Jane Eyre* (9,6)
9 Jane thinks she saw one of these wearing her wedding dress (5)
12 A child like Jane who's parents have died (6)
13 The surname under which *Jane Eyre* was originally written (4)
14 Rochester's lofty secret (6)
15 St. John Rivers became a missionary here (5)
21 To get married when you are married to someone else (6)
22 Surname of St. John, Mary and Diana (6)
27 Mrs. Reed suffered one of these when her son took his own life (6)
28 Deep affection (4)
30 Bertha Mason is this (3)

SPOT THE DIFFERENCE

TASK:

There are 10 differences between these pictures. Can you spot them?

COLOR ME IN

CHARLOTTE BRONTË - TRUE OR FALSE?
TEACHERS' VERSION

TRUE OR FALSE?	ANSWER:
Charlotte's father was a teacher in Yorkshire.	**False. He was a clergyman.**
Charlotte was an only child.	**False. She had five siblings.**
Charlotte lived for most of her life in Brussels.	**False. She spent less than two years in Brussels.**
Her first book was *Persuasion*.	**False. Her first book was *The Professor*. Her first published book was *Jane Eyre*.**
Brontë wasn't the family's real name.	**True. The family name was originally Brunty. Her father changed it to Brontë.**
There is a museum dedicated to the Brontës.	**True. The Brontë Parsonage Museum.**
Charlotte was first married when she was eighteen.	**False. She was 38 when she married.**
Charlotte used the pen name Currer Bell.	**True.**
Charlotte's middle name was Jane.	**False.**
Charlotte died when she was seventy years old.	**False. Charlotte was only thirty-eight when she died.**

CHARLOTTE BRONTË – RESEARCH TEMPLATE
TEACHERS' VERSION

QUESTION:	ANSWER:
Where and when was Charlotte Brontë born?	**April 21, 1816 at Thornton, Yorkshire.**
Whom did she marry?	**Arthur Bell Nichols.**
What was the name of her first novel? Written, not published.	***The Professor.***
What was the name of her second novel?	***Jane Eyre.***
Where did Charlotte live in February 1842?	**Brussels, the Pensionnat Heger.**
How much did Charlotte and her siblings pay to have *Poems* published?	**Around £50.**
How many copies did they sell in the first year?	**2.**
Who published Charlotte's biography in 1857?	**Elizabeth Gaskell.**
When was her novel *The Professor* first published?	**In 1857 posthumously.**
In which novel would you find Shirley Keeldar?	***Shirley*.**
Name all of Charlotte's novels.	***Jane Eyre*, *Shirley*, *Villette*, *The Professor*.**
Name Charlotte's siblings.	**Patrick Branwell, Emily Jane, Anne, Elizabeth, Maria.**

JANE EYRE
TEACHERS' VERSION

TASK 1:

Show on a map of the world which countries were the 1st, 2nd, 3rd and so on to allow all adults to vote.
http://en.wikipedia.org/wiki/Universal_suffrage

TASK 2:

Do the same exercise showing votes for women. This site tells all!!
www.bbc.co.uk/radio4/womanshour/timeline/votes_to_women.shtml

TASK 3:

Education was an issue for the poor too. Research education in Victorian times, and find answers to the following: -

Who funded schools In the UK in the Victorian era?
Church, private individuals, Board Schools, Ragged Schools.

Did working children receive any education at all?
Possible but variable and not compulsory.

Did standards differ between rural and urban communities?
This answer could encompass a variety of responses and still be "right"!

When were education acts passed making schooling compulsory? Varies by country.
www.spartacus.schoolnet.co.uk/education.htm

What are the legal requirements today? Varies by country. US latest is here.
http://en.wikipedia.org/wiki/Education_in_the_United_States

Who funds education now?
The state, some individual students or parents. Again, varies by country.

BACKGROUND RESEARCH
TEACHERS' VERSION

Answers in **bold**

TEST YOURSELF

1. Which country gave the vote to women first? France, Finland or England?
Finland.

2. When did the *Representation of the People Act* come into being?
1918.

3. When could women first stand in elections in the UK?
1907.

4. Which country was the first (of currently independent countries) to give the vote to women?
New Zealand.

5. Who began training for nurses in 1856?
Florence Nightingale.

6. Who wrote *The Princess*?
Alfred, Lord Tennyson.

7. Which bestseller of 1839 did Sarah Ellis write?
The Women of England.

8. Mary Wollstonecraft is the famous mother of which writer?
Mary Shelley.

9. When was The People's Charter first drafted?
1838.

10. In which year is Catholic Emancipation said to have taken place?
1829.

KNOW YOUR ABCs
TEACHERS' VERSION

Answers in **bold**

No.	Question	Answer
1	Jane Eyre went to work as a governess and taught Rochester's ward Adèle. This would indicate that Rochester was: a) poor b) rich c) in need of a babysitter	**B**
2	In 1901 the school leaving age was: a) 9 b) 10 c) 12	**C**
3	During the industrial revolution, there was a shift in the population from rural areas toward: a) towns and cities b) the seaside c) the mountains	**A**
4	Charlotte Brontë attended which school: a) She didn't attend school b) Parsonage Ragged School c) The Clergy Daughters' School	**C**
5	*Jane Eyre* was first published in 1847. Who was the reigning monarch at that time? a) Queen Victoria b) Queen Elizabeth I c) King William IV	**A**

UNDERSTANDING THE NOVEL
TEACHERS' VERSION

Answers in **bold**

TEST YOURSELF 2

1. Who proposes to Jane?
   St. John Rivers and Mr. Rochester.

2. What happened to Jane's parents?
   They died when Jane was a baby.

3. Which school did Jane attend?
   Lowood.

4. Name five locations in which the story takes place.
   Gateshead Hall, Lowood, Thornfield Hall, Moor House (or Marsh End), Ferndean.

5. Name all of the Rivers family.
   Diana, Mary, St. John.

6. What was the name of Rochester's dog?
   Pilot.

7. Where did Bertha come from?
   Jamaica.

8. Who was Mrs. Fairfax? And Adèle?
   Mr. Rochester's housekeeper at Thornfield.
   Mr. Rochester's ward.

9. Who was Rochester rumoured to be about to marry?
   Blanche Ingram.

10. What happens to St. John?
    He goes to India as a missionary.

JANE EYRE QUIZ
TEACHERS' VERSION

Answers in **bold**

1. Jane lives - until she is 10 - in
   (c) Gateshead.

2. Her first home is
   (d) the mansion of her uncle's family.

3. What is an apothecary?
   (a) A medical practitioner.

4. Aunt Reed promised her husband
   (b) to raise her as one of her own.

5. Lowood is
   (a) a charity school for female orphans.

6. Who is Jane's first close friend?
   (d) Helen Burns.

7. Which of the following characters says he might bend Jane "like a reed"?
   b) Rochester.

8. Which of the following elements is NOT represented in characters' names and/or natures?
   (b) Earth.

9. Who describes Jane as a "servant and agent" of Satan?
   (d) Brocklehurst.

10. Which of these descriptions best fits Jane?
    (d) "an independent woman...[her] own mistress"
    (this is an opinion – but also her own view).

11. Who says this to Rochester: "I have not been buried with inferior minds, and excluded from every glimpse of communion with what is bright and energetic and high...I have talked face to face with what I reverence...with an original, a vigorous, an expanded mind"?
    (a) Jane.

12. "The last letter I received from him drew from my eyes human tears, and yet filled my heart with Divine joy". What does Jane mean?
    (c) that she's sad St. John is dying but glad for him because he will get his "sure reward" in heaven.

YOU COULDN'T MAKE IT UP!
TEACHERS' VERSION

TASK 1:

Compare *Jane Eyre* to Charlotte's own life story. Find THREE major events in the life story that don't occur in the life and vice versa. Find THREE events that happened in both. (Caution – that second was partly a trick question).

Answer:

Any three from events clearly not reflected in the novel, including that Charlotte was not an orphan. She grew up in her own home with a mother (at first), siblings (three who lived into adulthood) and a father. She had two sisters who, like her, became famous Victorian novelists. She went to a school for the daughters of clergymen, not for orphans, and the epidemic that broke out there was TB, not typhus. She wrote more than painted. She had a brother who was a painter and who wrote books with her in childhood and whom she was distressed to lose when he died. She married a clergyman when she was about seventeen years older than Jane was when she married Rochester. She worked at Norton Conyers – which is a bit like Thornfield – but did not have a famous romance and marriage with its owner, nor find a "mad wife in the attic."

Any three from actual biography that reflect what is in the novel, including - Charlotte like Jane was raised by an aunt in a house with a boy and two girls. The boy she grew up with later died of addiction, dissipation and debauchery. She, like Jane, went away to school where an epidemic broke out and she lost a loved one (two in fact). Both worked as a governess. Both worked as teachers. Both had a passionate love affair with an older man – although the details of Charlotte's affair aren't clear. Both received proposals from a clergyman. Both were from Yorkshire and the impoverished gentry class. Both wrote a book drawing on many of these experiences, called *Jane Eyre: an Autobiography*.

The trick question is that of course none of *Jane Eyre* actually happened. It is all made up.

JANE
TEACHERS' VERSION

WORKSHEET 2 **Jane Eyre: a fairy tale heroine?**

Episode: location, description of episode and comments.	**Fairy tale or realism or both? Rate the episode 1-5 where 5 is total realism and 1 is total fairy tale. Explain your rating.**
Gateshead: (a) Jane is an orphan and a dependant in the house of a selfish, hard-hearted aunt, thrown upon the cruelty of relations who neglect and abuse her. Victorian society with its very high birth rates and very high death rates produced many more orphans than we have now. Orphans were one of the main issues of the age and a common subject of Victorian novels.	**(a) The rating should reflect the mixture of fairy tale and realism. As in a fairy tale, an orphan is bullied and abused, and we feel sorry and angry on her behalf. But she is a real girl with a real temper, not a little angel or a passive Cinderella, and the social (and all too common) Victorian reality of being an orphan – without rights – is clear. She is also not adorably pretty (or loved and pitied by the servants) and passive like a fairy tale orphan would be. (3?)**
(b) Locked in the "red room," with its "certain secret drawer in the wardrobe" (in which documents to do with Jane are hidden?) on a moonlit night, Jane sees her own spooky reflection in a looking-glass, "with a white face and arms specking the gloom and glittering eyes of fear moving where all else was still (like) a real spirit…one of the tiny phantoms, half fairy, half imp." And then – as her raging blood cools, believing "Mr. Reed's spirit" has returned to avenge her – "a gleam from a lantern" which "prepared as my mind was for horror…I thought…was a…vision from another world…I thought a ghost would come". She screams in terror, a scream that in turn terrifies her guards. But her (later, adult) narrator does not say it was a ghost, only that her child's mind believed it was.	**(b) Again, mixed, but nearer realism? The secret drawer has the fairy tale quality of a hidden identity. For example, Jane would "really" be a princess and the secret is locked up in a drawer. The letter and will that eventually bring her a fortune are hidden from her by Aunt Reed in just this magical way. But the drawer also suggests the psychological repressions of obligations – family love, etc. - toward Jane within Aunt Reed. The ghost visit is kept at arm's length by the adult narrator – we feel the child's terror strongly but don't believe in or fear the ghost ourselves. The half fairy/half imp Jane sees in the mirror is actually spookier: there is something genuinely ghostly about this child whose tale is being told to us by the adult she became. If there is a strong fairy tale element here, it is in the haunted mind-worlds of children and their imaginations. (3 or 4?)**
(c) Wakes up in front of a "terrible red glare, crossed with thick black bars" surrounded by "a hollow sound…as if muffled by a rush of wind or water… terror confused my faculties..(but) I was in my own bed, and...the red glare was the nursery fire." The description is like Victorian descriptions of hell: the child may believe she's gone there, but the adult narrator corrects this.	**(c) As above but more so? – this is a real narrative of a child being spooked, but we ourselves are outside of this imagined hell. Less a fairy tale, more a psychological study of childhood – and more a concern for her terror than a sharing of it. (4?)**
(d) "Shaking from head to foot, thrilled with ungovernable excitement," Jane retaliates after her aunt slanders her to Mr. Brocklehurst… "Mrs. Reed looked frightened…she was lifting up her hands,	**(d) Mixed, but as soon as we start seeing Jane herself as spooky, it becomes nearer a fairy tale. We have already seen inside this child's mind, and all the ghosts and specters and**

JANE
TEACHERS' VERSION

rocking herself to and fro, and even twisting her face as if she would cry. ...A ridge of lit heath, alive, glancing, devouring, would have been a meet emblem of my mind when I accused and menaced Mrs. Reed." Though Bessie prefers this new Jane and finds her less provoking than the "start" of the previously "queer, frightened, shy little thing" at being spoken to sharply, this rage expresses the Jane she has become: revengeful and superstitious and almost supernaturally threatening. A "discord at Gateshead Hall."	**terrors that lurk there. Now this real character – here called a "discord" – is shown as having something in her that can really scare (and haunt the conscience of?) an adult. Perhaps Aunt Reed's husband really has come back to haunt the house after all, but in the shape of Jane herself and all that is within her. A ridge of lit heath is a very powerful elemental force – rather like Bertha later – and though the self-destructive fire of this anger burns away to nothing and Jane therefore rejects it (as Bertha fails to do), this makes Jane a genuine mini "Bertha/spectre//mad wife in the attic"**
Lowood: this whole section has often been praised for its extreme realism. Many Victorian documents, as well as documentary novels, describe schools exactly like this. Can you find any "fairy tale" elements? Is there still a touch of Cinderella here?	**We may well read Lowood as a Cinderella fairy tale - the brutal privation of poor sweet little girls by a wicked man – but there were all too real Victorian charity schools like this. The Brontës went to one, and two of the girls died there. Also, the older girls aren't angels, (they steal food from the younger ones) – in fact only Helen actually is a "fairy tale" angel, mistreated and yet returning "good" for evil. Not all the teachers are equally heartless, and even the "nice" one (Miss Temple) is realistically limited in her "angel" (or "fairy godmother") powers. The adult narrator looks back in amusement as well as horror, and the "monster" (Mr. Brocklehurst) is partly laughable, even at the time, as he would be in a real school with real schoolgirls. (4 or 5?)**
Thornfield: find the following folk/fairy tale elements in Jane's experiences: a magical dog, a Prince, a fortune teller, a fairy tale proposal (one early reader called this "Conduct hardly proper between a single man and a maid in her teens"), a haunting, a vampire, a Bluebeard's wife, a visit to hell, a fairy godmother? In each case, is there also a realistic explanation? What is it? One has been completed for you.	(a) **There is what Jane calls a "foul German spectre, the vampyr" – it bites Mason in the attic and Jane actually has to nurse Mason afterwards until the light of dawn. There are other descriptions of the same creature in terms of devil and beast (find them yourselves). But before the days of "sectioning", dangerously insane family members of the upper classes were often secreted in remote mansions. One early reviewer wrote, "Neither is the mystery of Thornfield an exaggeration of reality. We, ourselves, know of a large mansion-house in a distant county where, for many years, a miscreant was kept in close confinement...only darkly hinted at in the neighbourhood." (H.F. Chorley, 1847).**

JANE
TEACHERS' VERSION

(b) The "Gytrash" (p. 108) – a magical dog/horse/mule that appears out of the dusk – is clearly present in Jane's memory of Bessie's tales and is transferred in her mind to her first momentous meeting with Rochester's horse and "great dog". There is an explanation but also a sense of haunting. (2 or 3?)

(c) Rochester is certainly a sort of fairy tale Prince – rich, romantic and with a sort of "castle" - coming mysteriously into Jane's life at dusk, changing her life and answering her heart's deepest wish. But he is also a real "Prince" – an aristocrat, described in some detail as such, with a real history, family background and fortune – and business to attend to. He is deliberately not Prince "handsome" in the fairy tale way. And in any case, is love not always in some sense where a fairy tale comes into real life? (3?)

(d) The fortune teller turns out to be as much a charade as everything else going on during the Ingram visit. (5)

(e) The proposal is in an orchard actually compared to "Eden" on midsummer eve in an English summer of "Italian" sunshine. It doesn't get much more fairy tale than this. The thunderbolt that destroys half the tree it happened under is also more like a tale from "romance" or even the Bible than realism – (except that hot weather does change like this in real life England and always seems too good to be true).

(f) The mysterious haunting by a specter or vampire and all the night-time screams are explained by the revelation that it was Bertha, the lunatic wife in the attic, though even this real-life, light-of-day explanation is spooky enough.

(g) Rochester is a Bluebeard insofar as he has a past of secret wives (or mistresses) concealed that his present wife will discover in a sequence of locked rooms. But he has not killed any of them, and only Bertha is actually his wife and concealed on the premises. More real than not, but more fairy tale atmosphere than most wives would want. (3 or 4?)

JANE
TEACHERS' VERSION

	(h) Jane is described as standing calm and quiet on the edge of hell. This is both real and fairy tale, and very powerfully so, because Bertha is associated with fire and sin and is both herself suffering hell and bringing it into Jane and Rochester's Eden. (2.5?) **(i) The "fairy godmother" could be the "mother" who says to Jane, "Daughter, flee temptation" and whom she answers "Mother, I will." But she doesn't actually appear as a person with a wand – she is more a metaphor for Jane's conscience – or God within? – guiding her away from the dangerous love and passion she feels for her beloved Rochester. (4 or 5?)**
Moor House/ Morton: Jane, by complete chance, and at death's door, stumbles in the middle of a remote moor upon long lost (and now – like her – orphaned) cousins who are the mirror reverse image of the Reeds. Then a fortune is left to Jane (Jane Heir) – at Christmas – by a long lost uncle. Out of the blue, she gets the ready–made family she's always lacked and independence. Fairy tale happy endings?	**Well, dream-come-true fortunes were made in the West Indies at this time, and sudden fortunes were left to long-lost family in real life as well as in novels. And not only does Jane's story not end – or become truly happy – she even keeps teaching at Morton school! So real life goes on after and in spite of the magical appearance of a family and fortune. Mixed. (3?)**
Ferndean: And they all lived happily ever after? Can you find any examples where Jane is clearly a real woman living in a real Victorian world rather than a fairy tale princess in fairy tale heaven? (Hint: would her husband have gotten a new hand and all his sight back in a traditional fairy tale?)	**Thornfield is wooded and summer-warm after Lowood's wintry cold and typhus spring, and this fits Jane's psychological state. Ferndean has some elements of Sleeping Beauty about it – Jane finds Rochester in and behind thick woods, kisses and revives him, and they marry, let their family know, have children and live happily ever after. (Surely they deserve it!) But the real problems don't all magically disappear. Rochester never fully recovers, Jane has parental responsibilities including Adèle's schooling that take some time to get right, and although she writes to St. John, he doesn't immediately respond or forgive. The last paragraph is more realistically troubling than a fairy tale ending, and it suggests real life relationships and problems can't quite be settled by a fairy tale closure– though it doesn't cloud Rochester and Jane's companionship. Fairy tale-ish, but all narrative closure has to be a little bit like this. (2 or 3?)**

THE REEDS
TEACHERS' VERSION

TASK 1:

Group Discussion

Aunt Reed is a weak parent who lets her "darling" son have his own way. She does not make him go to school and indulges his "violent tyrannies," gluttony and rages. "He twisted the necks of the pigeons, killed the pea chicks, set the dogs at the sheep, stripped the hothouse vines of their fruit, and broke the buds off the choicest plants in the conservatory: he called his mother 'old girl'… bluntly disregarded her wishes … tore her silk attire." In the end, this weakness destroys both of them. John is never disciplined and – unlike Jane – and like his sisters – develops no inner strength or self-discipline. He later kills himself – by way of debt, jail, addiction, and "strange ways," hastens his mother's early death and wastes a good deal of the family fortune. Jane complains that Eliza is "headstrong and selfish" and yet is "respected" rather than corrected. Georgina is spoiled, spiteful and insolent and is "indulged." Her beauty "purchases indemnity for every fault." (Eliza ends by "walling herself up alive" in a convent, and Georgina sells herself for a society marriage. "Georgiana made an advantageous match with a wealthy worn out man of fashion; and…Eliza actually took the veil." Both appear to be like reeds in the wind, Eliza bending to one extreme, Georgina to the other. Again in complete contrast to Jane who insists on her own self-determination, "I resisted all the way," they leave it to others to give their lives the structure they lack, eventually choosing one of the only two respectable Victorian options for ladies. Their fate has been set by their weak parenting.) Aunt Reed sets the tone in all of this for the whole household, including the servants, to follow, as of course they do. The only person Aunt Reed is strict with is Jane, who naturally feels she doesn't deserve it.

TASK 2:

Comprehension and Debate

1. Fat, bad skin, podgy, double-chinned face "thick lineaments in a spacious visage"
2. He "gorged himself habitually at table" and was sent too many cakes from home.
3. Can't find Jane when she hides – Eliza points her out to him. "dim and bleared eye" "not quick either of vision or conception" "blind and deaf on the subject"
4. Jane's vision is more by suggestion: she was up in the window and eyrie is the name of an eagle's nest – is she eagle-eyed / sharp in understanding? "I really saw in him a tyrant"?
5. Any 3 from: John never gets punished for any wrongdoing. He calls his mother "old girl." Georgina is "indulged"; "her pink cheeks and golden curls…purchase indemnity for every fault". Eliza is respected though selfish and headstrong. Jane is always at fault whatever she does. Aunt Reed manages her house and servants well, but her children – at times – defy and laugh at her authority. Jane is reported as a liar to Brocklehurst when it is Georgina who lies. When Jane finally confronts her, she is so obviously rattled, she caves in and says she wants to be her friend, then excludes her forever.
6. Self-knowledge and the courage of her convictions. "I am not deceitful …Deceit is not my fault… How dare I …because it is the truth." She grows out of the promise never to visit Aunt Reed when she is older: "Forgive me for my passionate language; I was a child then" – that was more anger than real strength – but she has the strengths of honesty and the courage of her convictions all her life.
7. Any general points about the indulged and indulgent life of a son of the wealthy gentry – our equivalent of a modern student but with lots of money – Rochester says he was dissipated but not debauched, whereas John's debauchery (addictions, gambling etc) are clear.

THE REEDS
TEACHERS' VERSION

8. Neither Georgiana nor Eliza obeys her mother's dying wish to send for Jane until she repeats it constantly. The sisters bicker about Edwin Vere and jealousy over Georgiana's social ambitions, and they plan their divergent futures while they wait for their mother to die. They have "nothing in common: they never had had." They have no intention of seeing each other again and actually prefer Jane's company to each other's. Georgiana frets about how bored she is, wishing for an invitation up to relatives in London. Eliza stitches for three hours and reads a prayer book for another three, spending less time with her mother than Jane does. Eliza's physical response to the death – "a spasm constricted her mouth for an instant: as it passed away she turned and left the room…[and did not drop] a tear" is as far as it gets. Georgiana bursts into "loud weeping" but doesn't even go in to see the corpse and afterwards dreads being left alone with Eliza and hurries away to London.
9. Eliza "walls herself alive in a convent" (i.e. becomes a nun); Georgiana marries a worn-out old man of fashion.

TASK 3:

Any sound argument based on the evidence that Aunt Reed's lack of firmness and correcting principle has actually led to John's debauchery, Eliza's sterile self-absorption and Georgiana's spoilt reliance on her prettiness.

BROCKLEHURST AND ST. JOHN RIVERS
TEACHERS' VERSION

Brocklehurst

As a child looking up at him he appears to Jane as "a black pillar." In Bessie's song "Kind angels only/ Watch o'er the steps of the poor orphan's child," but Brocklehurst only has time for hell and punishment. If there are angels among the "starved arms wrapped in pinafores" and "burnt porridge" of Brocklehurst's Lowood, they are Helen Burns and Miss Temple's warm fire and cake. But the latter is limited, and Helen's angel never really comes to earth.

Brocklehurst frightens Jane with hell but has no understanding of how a child thinks. He cannot see how the little boy he rewards with two gingerbread nuts for saying he prefers learning a verse from the Psalms to a nut, is doing it for the nuts. (And learning the same kind of hypocrisy Brocklehurst lives by.) And when he asks the honest-speaking Jane for the correct theory of what she must do to avoid hell, she says (with accidental comedy) "not die."

St. John

If Brocklehurst is a "black pillar" and "the black marble clergyman" St. John is "white marble," a "cold cumbrous column …gloomy and out of place…at the (Christmas) fireside." Like Brocklehurst, St. John's Christianity is stony and loveless. Unlike him, St. John is "of the grand order of men" (as grand in a different way as Rochester), "a warrior-priest, cool and inflexible as death," a calm heart and an unquiet spirit, without love for creatures of flesh and blood (even Rosamond), dreaming only of martyrdom and the conquest of eternal salvation.

But his devotion to duty is something very powerful (however repulsive and hard) in Jane's eyes – she herself gives up love in the same way as St. John does: for duty. St. John's religion is suicide – the solving of the problems of the world by denying and rejecting it altogether, rather than learning to control it. The exaltation of St. John's guiding prayer excites Jane – "religion called – angels beckoned – God commanded… death's gates opening showed eternity beyond." But when she asks for God's voice at the final moment, she hears Rochester's. The world – which God created – calls her back, and "my soul rushed out in gratitude at His feet." The world is not defeated by denying its existence.

HELEN BURNS AND MISS TEMPLE
TEACHERS' VERSION

TASK 1:

Poignantly, Helen is Jane's first friend and sibling/companion. With the possible exception of Bessie, Helen is the first positive human contact the ten-year-old orphan Jane ever has. Helen makes her feel welcome and tells her all about Lowood and, like Jane, is a favorite of Miss Temple. But Helen seems doomed to ill treatment by teachers, and we share Jane's irritation that she does not stand up for herself more, even if Jane learns that it is better to wait for Miss Temple to clear her name, than repeat the mistake of her tantrums at Aunt Reed. But Helen seems almost to want to be badly treated. She almost seeks death. In this, she is the same kind of Christian, more interested in heaven than earth, as St. John. Like Jesus she turns the other cheek even if her own life is at stake. When Helen becomes mortally ill, she is literally in another "place" from Jane, and when Jane is determined to see her, we wonder where their friendship has been in the meantime. Helen is literally "too good for this world". No doubt Jane learns self-control and fortitude and a practical submissiveness to hardship from Helen. She learns not to take herself at the world's valuation or to use that valuation to strengthen her own moral sense. But Helen was worth saving. She spends her last night on earth with Jane but not the previous months. Jane wakes up to find Helen Burns dead and herself alive. There is a terrible shock conveyed here, and the improvement of Lowood, though connected to Helen's "sacrifice" (along with the others who died) only partly compensates for it. Jane remembers her much later, out of the blue, at another death bed (Aunt Reed's), this context associating her – for the reader – once more with death rather than with life. "Whither will that spirit – now struggling to quit its material tenement – flit when at length released." It is as if the transcendent love Jane feels for Helen is always at the edge of life, the love of another world, as is the relationship she still has with St. John in the final paragraph of the novel. (And as, perhaps, Brontë has with one or more of her own lost siblings and loved ones?) (See also under language).

When the Rev. Brocklehurst lectures Miss Temple about scandalously putting "bread and cheese instead of burnt porridge, into these children's mouths, you ...little think how you starve their immortal souls" her face, "naturally pale as marble...closed as if it would have required a sculptor's chisel to open it...petrified severity." She is right and reasonable to resist Brocklehurst's evangelical ravings – which justify meanness and the starving of children – but her stoniness is a precursor of St. John's. Miss Temple teaches Jane reason and is caring of her girls in a restrained and reasonable way – and she later appears to have been a real companion at a certain level – the deepest Lowood can offer – but she does not return the near adult Jane's later deeper longing for warmth and love. For that, she needs someone quite different!

NARRATIVE
TEACHERS' VERSION

TASKS 1 AND 2:

Credit any grasp of the impact of point of view on how even real-life events are narrated, and the demonstration of this grasp in their own writing.

TASK 3:

Can you find evidence of Bertha's Creole background possibly being used as a shock device for Brontë's mainly white Victorian readers?

She is described as "having fearful blackened inflation of the lineaments" and having "lips swelled and dark."

WORD PATTERNS IN JANE EYRE
TEACHERS' VERSION

TASK 1:

Rochester and Fairfax are the names of two famous generals who fought on opposite sides in the English Civil War.

Many names relate to fire and/or water. Helen Burns combines both – a "burn" is a Yorkshire name for a stream. The names of both sets of Jane's cousins – Rivers and Reed – relate to water. Grace Poole not only combines in her name the idea of water and God (baptism?) but also guards the fiery and fire-starting Bertha. Grace often carries a rather prosaic tankard of ale – fluid again – but a fluid that (occasionally) prevents her damping down the fiery Bertha. Even the pronunciation of St. John's name (which sounds like "sin-jin") is suggestive – singeing rivers, ambiguous – both fire and water – like the other genuinely saintly character, Helen Burns.

TASK 2:

Heat/warmth and wet/coolness run through the book. Rochester, when dangerously passionate and alone with Jane in the middle of the night, has "strange fire in his look," and the fact that first his bed and later his entire house are set aflame by the over-passionate Bertha suggests that passion without control can be a destructive, injurious and even life-threatening force.

Nevertheless the absence of love is represented throughout the book in metaphors and similes of coldness (and often water): the miserable and lonely opening of the novel in "cold winter wind" and "penetrating rain," the red room Jane is sent to, and the whole atmosphere of Jane's life at Gateshead are cold. The misery of Jane's first months at Lowood are colder still, considering the misery of a Yorkshire moor winter in poorly heated rooms, and they are overseen by a man who is like a black pillar of stone. Too, after the dangerous but homely fire of Rochester, St. John's eye is like ice. Elsewhere, St. John is described in terms of unfeeling marble, which is a very cold stone.

TASK 3:

Three characters have clearly religious names: Miss Temple (whom the Lowood girls, including Jane, worship), Grace Pool and St. John Rivers. In every case, there is some reserve about these characters, and religion in the novel is both very important to Jane and regarded with some suspicion. Brontë's father was a clergyman, and all her own marriage proposals were received from clergymen. Her character, Jane, rejects the clergyman and marries the (reformed) rake. Later, Brontë accepts a clergyman. Miss Temple gives her some rare warmth and companionship during her teens – she is never quite as lonely at Lowood as she was at Gateshead – once she grows nearer adulthood. This is not the passionate warmth and love she needs (and which Miss Temple leaves to find in marriage – to yet another clergyman – anyway). For that she needs to leave Lowood (and the world of teenage hero worship and female friendship?) and enter Thornfield, the world of a man. Grace Poole is neither graceful nor endearing. She is a rough and humdrum creature whom Jane misinterprets for most of her time at Thornfield as the beast in the attic. In fact, she is the (sometimes unreliable) jailer of that beast. If she represents "grace" in any sense, it is as the guard over what Bertha represents: lusts, rages, animal drives. This "grace" could be that part of religion – the conscience – which is moral and stern, if not very inspiring or heart-touching or even very interesting: a necessary routine. And some preachers of the St. John and especially the Brocklehurst type talk of "grace" in that way, rather than as something beautiful and overwhelming. Brocklehurst says Julia Severn should be a child of "grace," not nature – in other words her hair shouldn't curl, even though it curls by nature. This is dreary, like Grace Poole. Perhaps we are supposed to feel the "grace" represented by Grace Poole as a necessary control but not a happy one on our nature, an appropriate brake to Bertha's case, if not Julia's. Perhaps her rather comical failure to guard Thornfield from Bertha when lulled with alcohol is a reminder of how our moral

WORD PATTERNS IN JANE EYRE
TEACHERS' VERSION

religion – our conscience as taught by strict Christianity – can fail, like the cautionary tales about binge drinking so popular nowadays. But she certainly doesn't have or spread any fun or even much respect from Jane or the reader.

Some critics even suggest that Charlotte Brontë's secret sympathies are with the passionate Bertha rather than the grim Grace Poole – just as they are with Julia Severn's nature rather than Brocklehurst's grace. This has to be squared with the destructive force of Bertha's fire when compared with Grace's "poole" – her metaphorical pouring of cold water on Bertha's passion – but it is true there is not a total vote in favor of this religiously named character either. It is easy to see why a section of the book's original critics felt the book to be uncouth and irreligious (even if they usually concentrated on her rejection of St. John in favor of Rochester).

St. John is the third religiously named character. And once again, the text (though intriguingly it ends with him) does not create a straightforward or positive attitude to him. He is certainly saintly. He literally sacrifices himself in the service of others at the end of the book. He is not a hypocrite like Brocklehurst, and the contrast of the two kinds of stoniness is significant. Brocklehurst is like a black pillar, and while we never see any violence or moral corruption (Victorian novels could only imply such things), there is something cringing about the way he visits and kow tows to the rich Mrs. Reed – and something intrusive if not downright creepy about the way he inspects the girls' stockings on the Lowood washing lines. St. John, by contrast, is like white marble. He is snowy white in his personal morality. Indeed, "pure as the driven snow" would describe him well: he "woos" Jane (if that is the word) in the snowy rivered mountains and is both as morally stainless and as cold as snow. His absolute moral purity – and his absolute commitment to his Christian mission and to selfless service – are towering achievements. If the Bible warns of whited sepulchres, and if literature is full of such hypocrites – white on the surface, rotten and stinking within – St. John is a unique creation in literature, and very rare in life. Jane refers to him as an extraordinary "being" – as if he were not quite human. He is white all through. Jane admires him almost as much as she fears him, and it is because of this admiration that she does fear and almost – even she, the original fighter – surrenders to him at the last, after all she's been through, knowing it would kill her. But he is nevertheless a tyrant, a whited version of John Reed. He does not love her – in fact he loves Rosamond Oliver but despises that fact, and Jane knows this. And Jane needs love, to both give and receive it. This – what a woman needs – was a radical statement then, and perhaps it still is. St. John, like many Victorians, assumed a woman could get along without it. The assertion, by both Jane and Diana, that Jane would die as a result, is not merely a physical statement about Jane's health in India. It is a representation, perhaps, of the fate of thousands of Victorian women, stranded and unloved in the missions (and agendas) their husbands' careers and lives launched them on.

TASK 4:

The heat of India is a very interesting aspect of this. St. John, who burns with divine mission but who in human terms is cold, ends up in a place too hot for his human body to live. Helen dies in Lowood as it finally melts towards spring and goes to a "better" place, out of the spiritual cold. But she lived all her earthly life in that cold.

In a book where warmth is associated with love and lonely coldness with its absence, "singeing" rivers with his marble cheek is forcing Jane into a world of such intense heat that she will die. St. John's love is a supernatural kind, the love of martyrs, a love that burns for God alone. But to Jane this is merely death – not the death of her self in love, but death without love, a life bereft of love, wilfully thrown away. Jane settles for earthly and human love – a perfect and romantic marriage of equals – specifically guided by God to do so. Nevertheless, for all that, the book ends with St. John burning away – toward a calm and holy death – in

WORD PATTERNS IN JANE EYRE
TEACHERS' VERSION

spiritual love, sacrificing himself for Jesus in India. His is not the only storyline that ends in burning death. Bertha burns to death in the passionate hell – or for Rochester the purgatory – of Thornfield. It is better to marry than to burn, says St. Paul in the Bible, (meaning marriage is a place where lust may be controlled). But fire is a very subtle metaphor throughout *Jane Eyre*. It can represent many kinds and degrees of love, not all of them desirable, but all perhaps better than the coldness of snow, marble, black pillars, Lowood and Gateshead.

Many of these patternings meet in the name and character of Helen Burns.
Consider what part this small, doomed but potent character plays in the overall patterning of the book. Her name (like St. John's) is both fire and water, flame and river. The New Testament includes the metaphor of a "baptism of fire." This is the Holy Ghost replacing the river as a means of baptism in a supernatural empowering of the disciples after Pentecost (Whitsun). Helen's name includes both levels. Part of her (like St. John) is already in a world beyond this one, and death is merely (to her) a happy way of going fully on to it. "Burns" is certainly a fiery name – there is no doubt that in the cold of Lowood, she is out of her natural element – but (despite the life-giving warmth of her friendship with the lonely Jane) "burns" conveys danger and pain rather than warmth. Some of this intensity returns at a more advanced and more mature level when the (now loved but again isolated) Jane meets St. John. Both Helen and St. John die, too good for this world, but they are by no means easily lost to Jane. Both these fire-water named characters are very important to her and the overall currents of the text. They provide another dimension and frame to Jane's ultimate tale of earthly happiness.

Death (and religion) was, as we have seen, much more present in Victorian lives than ours. And it is reasonable to assume that some of Brontë's own grief at losing her two sisters at Cowan Bridge, not to mention her mother, went into the creation of this poignant and wistful character. But it is how the character works within this text that we must gauge. I suggest that, for all the nobility of Helen's Christian character, in a very real sense Jane rejects Helen, and her love of death, just as she rejects St. John. Jane wants to live.

ADVANCED STRUCTURAL PATTERNS IN *JANE EYRE*
TEACHERS' VERSION

The Sisters

The sisters are one example of the opposites/balanced extremes pattern. Each pairing has an active sister and a passive one. A variation is that both Brocklehurst ladies (and their mother too for that matter) are passive – like one person. The passive (paler) sister is called Mary – the traditional name and role of the archetypal "good" woman? – in both Ingram and Rivers pairings. The Rivers sisters are certainly an improvement on the Reeds and are a real family for Jane, but just as St. John is still a problem brother (though better than the anti-saintly John Reed), so Jane's relationship with her Rivers sisters is either as pupil (as with Miss Temple and, more terrifyingly, with St. John) or teacher (as with Adèle and the Morton girls): not the balanced blend of giving and receiving she finally achieves with Rochester.

THE PLOT THICKENS EVEN FURTHER!
TEACHERS' VERSION

TASK 2:

Jane in the red room prefigures Bertha in the attic, and we see this in that order, rather than seeing Bertha in the attic first. In fact in real time, Bertha – who has been in the attic in Thornfield for 10 years – was already there, and in some similar attic in the West Indies, before Jane ever went into the red room, but the plot never encourages us to speculate on this – the plot shows us Jane first, and then Bertha much later, – at a later stage of Jane's life – a time when Jane has – perhaps – grown beyond the need of such savage imprisonment or learned enough cunning and self-control to avoid it. The way that the Rivers family of Diana, Mary and St. John are plotted as a reflection – and mirror opposite – of the Reed family of Eliza, Georgiana and St. John – is another example of foreshadowing or recapitulation. The plot presents us with the better family second, and taking Jane in rather than throwing her out, in a deliberate comparison and contrast of the two story lines. Jane is on both occasions an outcast, an orphan at Gateshead and effectively an orphan again at Moor House. The plot could have shown us the latter story first and contrasted the earlier tale as a flashback. But this would have spoiled the sense of Jane having made some real progress in her life. The plot could easily have avoided the comparison – it goes to great lengths to draw it and stretches realism towards fairy tale to do so – but creates a mirror structure of the two events. The Rivers are what the Reeds could have been and vice versa.

BRONTË – PAINTER WITH WORDS?
TEACHERS' VERSION

It is difficult to avoid talking about Brontë without using a metaphor of painting. Like many Victorian painters, Brontë "painted" her portraits and stories against and into landscapes of wild natural beauty and power: moors, mountains and rivers, typically the stormy and weather-beaten Yorkshire landscapes she knew. The Romantic style of painting popular in the period – natural, vivid, elemental, pulsating with energy – is often not only the setting of the story but in some ways the story itself. The thunderbolt on Midsummer Eve is a romantic painting in words. The elements which flow through the story – fire, water, and air – are reflected in the very names of the characters – e.g. Burns, Rivers, Eyre etc. And the use of colors in the patterning of the story and the relationships works like a Romantic painting. Red (for the positive warmth of life and company and the dangerous heat of passion) and its contrast with white (the negative cold of control, loneliness and death) is a constant pattern in the book. Even before the famous red room, on the first page of the novel, we have the quotation (singled out by G.H. Lewes) contrasting the scarlet drapery with the white mist and cloud above. This extract is swiftly followed by associations between frost and snow…death white realms… and the cold and ghastly moon. Brontë gives colors – here white – the kind of artistic value that a painter especially prizes.

JANE EYRE WORD SEARCH
TEACHERS' VERSION

Solution:

LOWOOD (1)	RED ROOM (1)	BERTHA (4)	PILOT (2)
ROCHESTER (1)	HORSE (8)	FIRE (6)	WIFE (5)
HELEN BURNS (3)	BLANCHE(1)	JANE EYRE (2)	GHOST (1)
RIVERS (5)	JOHN REED (4)	LOVE (2)	ATTIC (2)
ORPHAN (2)	MAD (7)	BRONTE (3)	THORNFIELD (2)

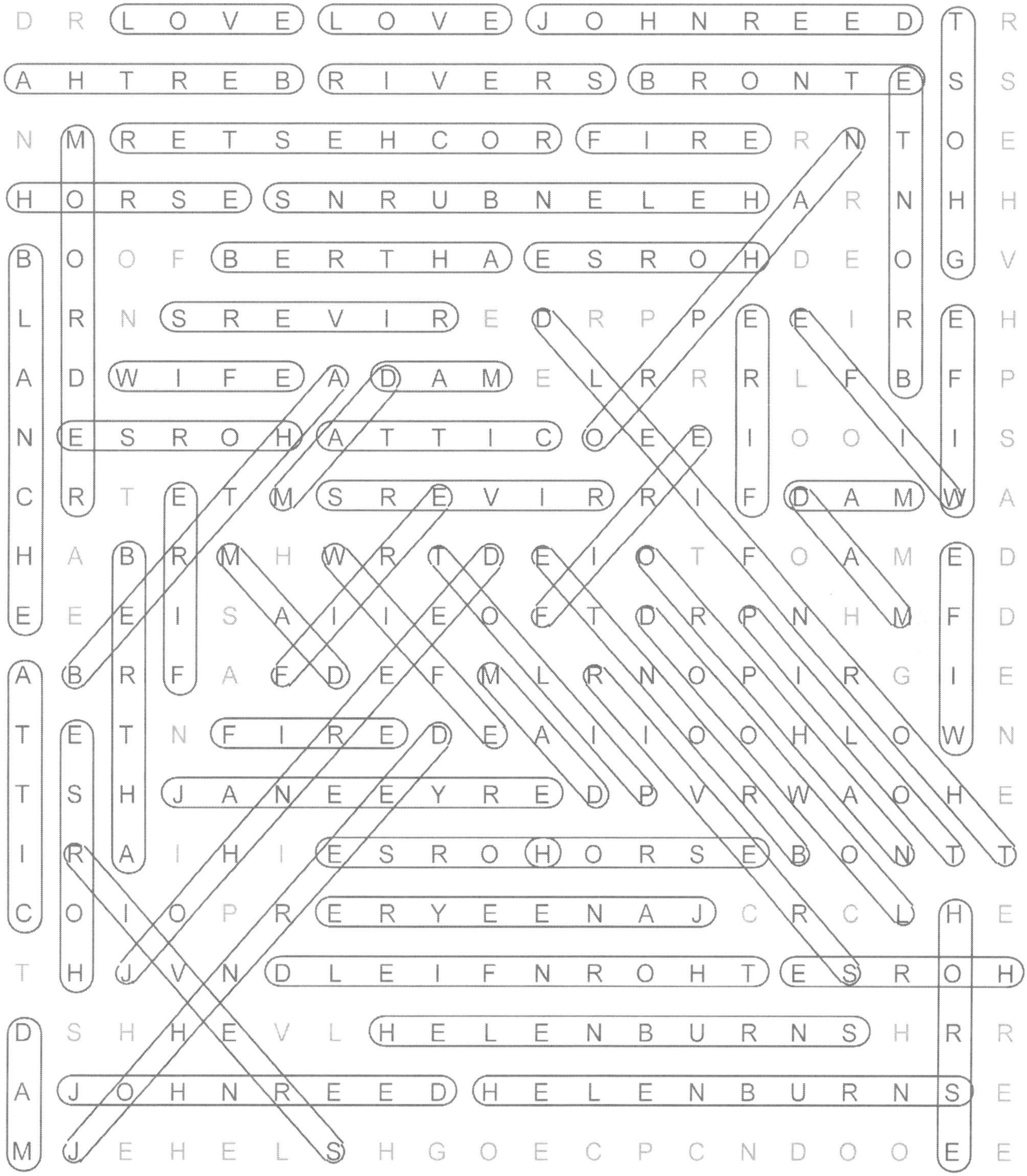

JANE EYRE WORD SEARCH
TEACHERS' VERSION

Solution:

RED ROOM (4)	SCORN (6)	JOHN REED (2)	HELEN BURNS(3)
BLANCHE (6)	MADEIRA (7)	GEORGIANA (2)	FERNDEAN (5)
GOVERNESS (4)	THORNFIELD HALL (2)	RIVERS (7)	CLERGYMAN (3)
TYPHUS (7)	MAGISTRATE (1)	CHARADES (5)	LOWOOD (10)
CANDLESTICK (6)	MISSIONARY (4)	ROCHESTER (4)	BRONTE (10)

JANE EYRE CROSSWORD
TEACHERS' VERSION

SPOT THE DIFFERENCE
TEACHERS' VERSION

EDUCATIONAL WEBSITE LINKS

PROMOTING LITERACY IN THE CLASSROOM:-

Graphic Novels for Multiple Literacies

www.readingonline.org/newliteracies/jaal/11-02_column/

In an increasingly visual culture, literacy educators can profit from the use of graphic novels in the classroom, especially for young adults. Educators need not worry that graphic novels discourage text reading. Lavin (1998) even suggested that reading graphic novels might require more complex cognitive skills than the reading of text alone. **Gretchen E. Schwarz**

The Graphic Classroom

http://graphicclassroom.blogspot.com/

The Graphic Classroom is a resource for teachers and librarians to help them stock high quality, educational-worthy, graphic novels and comics in their classroom or school library.

Graphic novels - engaging readers and encouraging literacy

www.ltscotland.org.uk/literacy/findresources/graphicnovels/index.asp

The showcase resource highlights how graphic novels can be used throughout the curriculum.

Learning and Teaching Scotland

Graphic Novels across the curriculum

www.ltscotland.org.uk/literacy/images/Graphic%20novels%20across%20the%20curriculum_tcm4-402928.doc

The flexibility of the comic medium means that it can be used to tell stories in a simple way, without the reader appearing "uncool." However, this same flexibility means that the comic can also tell phenomenally complex stories or explain difficult ideas. This is a medium, rather than a genre, and can be used to create demanding texts across a range of genres. **Mel Gibson**

Expanding Literacies through Graphic Novels

www.readwritethink.org/lessons/lesson_view.asp?id=1102

Gretchen Schwarz offers a rationale, based on the need for current students to learn multiple literacies, for the use of graphic novels in the high school English class. She highlights several titles, suggests possible classroom strategies, and discusses some of the obstacles teachers may face in adding graphic novels to their curriculum. **Gretchen E. Schwarz**

Eek! Comics in the Classroom!

www.education-world.com/a_curr/profdev/profdev105.shtml

More and more teachers are finding that once-maligned comics, and their big brothers graphic novels, can be effective tools for teaching a multitude of literacy skills to students with a variety of learning needs. **Education World**

Using Comics and Graphic Novels in the Classroom

www1.ncte.org/store/books/126835.htm?source=gs

As teachers, we're always looking for new ways to help our students engage with texts. James Bucky Carter and the contributors to this collection have found an effective approach: use graphic novels!

The National Council of Teachers of English (NCTE)

Getting graphic! Using graphic novels to promote literacy with pre teens and teens

http://findarticles.com/p/articles/mi_m0PBX/is_4_38/ai_n6123048

Getting Graphic! also tackles the big question: are graphic novels, aka comic books, "junk literature for children," or do they have a "cultural and educational value and belong on the shelves of libraries across the nation"? **Michele Gorman**

EDUCATIONAL WEBSITE LINKS

Comics in Education
www.humblecomics.com/comicsedu/

The potency of the picture story is not a matter of modern theory but of anciently established truth. Before man thought in words, he felt in pictures. **Gene Yang**

Going Graphic - Comics at Work in the Multilingual Classroom
http://college.heinemann.com/shared/onlineresources/E00475/chapter2.pdf

Theory, research, practice, guidelines and resources for using comics and graphic novels in the classroom. **Stephen Cary**

Graphic Novels and Curriculum Integration
http://members.shaw.ca/yaying/518final/integ.html

"Introducing graphic novels that address history, politics, literature, or social issues in a comic style format into the school library or classroom may begin to help to bridge the gap between what students want and what schools require." **ESL Teaching in Canada**

Information for Teachers and Teacher-Librarians
www.informationgoddess.ca/Comics&GraphicNovels/teachers&tls.htm

Are you interested in resources for teaching your students:
- more about visual literacy?
- how to interpret the finer point of visual texts?
- how to produce their own comics? **(Canadian website)**

Comic Books for Young Adults - A Guide for Librarians
http://library.buffalo.edu/libraries/asl/guides/graphicnovels/

"As educators become increasingly aware of the importance of different learning styles, it is clear that comic books can be a powerful tool for reaching visual learners." **Michael R Lavin**

Graphic Novels - a visual literary art form
www.clermont.lib.oh.us/teensite/teengraphicnov.html

What is most exciting is that a picture language and a word language can interweave, which can't be done by either one alone." **Will Eisner, Clermont County Public Library**

The Secret Origin of Good Readers
www.night-flight.com/secretorigin/index.html

Discusses how teachers, librarians, retailers, and publishers can work together to bring comic books into the classroom for use as an innovative and motivating cross-curricular teaching tool and a vehicle for promoting reading and literacy.

GENERAL GRAPHIC NOVEL SITES:-

Graphic Novel Review Site for Teens
www.noflyingnotights.com

Covers everything from superheroes to historical novels via Manga and cartoons. **Robin Brenner**

Comics Worth Reading
http://comicsworthreading.com

Independent Opinions by Johanna Draper Carlson and friends
News and reviews of graphic novels, manga, comic books, and related subjects.

EDUCATIONAL WEBSITE LINKS

MAKING COMICS AND GRAPHIC NOVELS:-

National Association of Comic Art Educators
www.teachingcomics.org

One of the primary the goals of NACAE is to assist educational institutions and individual educators interested in establishing a comics art curriculum. Excellent links, and papers on the topic of Comics in the Classroom. **NACAE**

Scrap Comics
http://escrapbooking.com/projects/scrapcomic/index.htm

"Let's use picture books, sequential art, and comics as tools for teaching critical thinking skills related to sequencing across the curriculum." **Eduscapes**

Comic Life
http://plasq.com/comiclife

Lets you create comics, beautiful picture albums, how-to's... and more! Can be used on whiteboards with electronic copies of the books in this series.

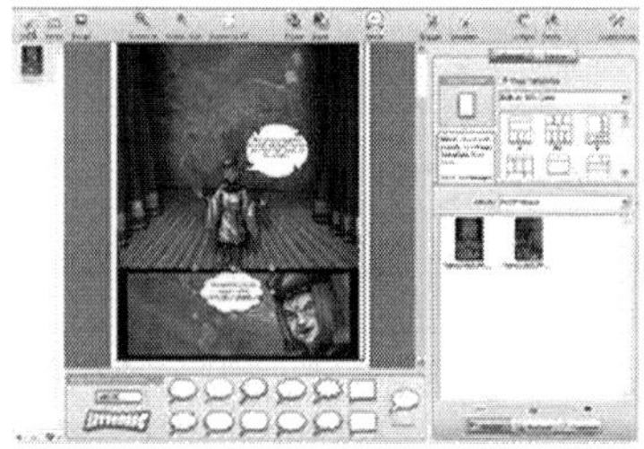

BRONTË RELATED SITES AND ORGANIZATIONS

Brontë Parsonage Blog
www.bronteparsonage.blogspot.com

The Brontë Parsonage Museum and Brontë Society
www.bronte.info

Chronology of Charlotte Brontë's Life
www.umd.umich.edu/casl/hum/eng/classes/434/charweb/BRONTECH.htm

Charlotte Brontë: A Brief Biography
www.victorianweb.org/authors/bronte/cbronte/brontbio.html

A site dedicated to the Brontës
www.thebrontes.net/

The Life of Charlotte Brontë by Elizabeth Gaskell (1857)
www.lang.nagoya-u.ac.jp/~matsuoka/EG-Charlotte-1.html

The full book, chapter by chapter.